# Confident

# Hope

Getting Through
What You're Going Through

## Hope for the Hopeless

*"Rejoice in our confident hope. Be patient in trouble,
and keep on praying." (Romans 12:12)*

When facing death, divorce, disabilities, drugs,
devastating relationships, or a dismal financial
future, you can still experience
CONFIDENT HOPE!

*All Scripture references are from the New Living Translation. Boldface
and bracketed portions are added for my emphasis or comments.*

# Bob Goshen

# DEDICATION

This is a special book dedicated to my children and grandchildren and my beautiful wife Kay.

To my wonderful children—Ami Goshen, Ashlee Goshen Hope, and Rob Goshen. Having the opportunity to watch my kids grow has been so rewarding. I believe all parents can choose to focus on either the good or bad in their children. I wish only to remember the good times, the times of love, laughter, and just being together. As parents, it would be easy to find fault in our kids, to focus on where we have been disappointed. I'm sure our parents could have done the same. But as we begin to get older and enter the fourth quarter of life, we realize that the greatest gift we have received is our children. So to Ami, Ashlee, and Rob, thanks for the great memories, the smiles, and the constant love you have given to both your mother and me. Your futures are bright, but you will encounter tunnels. When you hit a tunnel, run back to this book and be reassured that God is in control and you will make it through the dark times to brighter times.

Also, thank you for the gift of your children, our wonderful grandchildren. We now have 6 (I am confident that is the final count): Caleb (the only boy of the group), Kyleigh, McKenzie, Mikayla, Alexia, and Allison. At this writing their ages go from 14 down to 6. I have to say, it is great watching these young ones grow. Hearing their questions and, more important, their comments about life and their parents is amusing.

As I watch them, I am reminded of their parents as children, and I feel we've been granted a second chance to influence a generation. This is amazing! To you little ones, soon to become big ones, the future holds two choices. One choice is to follow

God and a set of moral values; the other is to follow the concepts of the world, the culture that has immorality as a standard. Your Nana and Papi had to make choices, hundreds of choices during our youth, and now hundreds more in our adult lives. As you can see by reading this book, some of my choices were incorrect, and as a result, I experienced turmoil in my life. I wish I could be in your brains 24 hours a day for the rest of your lives, whispering my thoughts to help you along the way as you are presented with your choices. Since that it not possible, I pray you will find time as you get older to read this book and to pull it out and reread as your tunnels come along.

To my kids and grandchildren, focus on values and moral choices, and even when you hit your tunnels God will show you through.

To my Katie: Wow, what an adventure we have had! Our lives have been amazing. We could create a movie that folks would love as they followed where we have been and what we have witnessed. What is amazing to me is how you stayed with me when you should have left, supported me when you should have quit, and loved me when I was not so loveable. As we have gone through our many tunnels thus far, it has been your faith and spirit that kept me moving when some would quit. You were a constant "cheerleader" even when you witnessed my dreadful mistakes. I have received nothing but belief and support during our entire marriage, and I know without a doubt that any success that has been accomplished is because of you. How can you let someone down who totally believes in you? You can't! As we move forward in life, do not put down your "pom poms," for we have more to explore, more to enjoy, and more to give. I love you baby! .........Papi/Bobby

# CONTENTS

# ACKNOWLEDGEMENTS

To my lovely wife, Kay, who has been by my side for 51 years. She lived this book with me—through each story she has felt the pain and the glory as we watched God fulfill his purpose. Kay has been my rock as we have traveled down the rails together going in and out of tunnels. I pray every man would have a wife like Kay, a spiritual giant, true helpmate, and prayer warrior. Love you honey.

My children: Rob, Ashlee, and Ami. What a blessing they have been over the years. Each has had to endure multiple tunnels, and they have found their strength in the Lord during each trial. Watching our children grow through challenging times has blessed me and Kay knowing they will always return to their Lord and Savior in their tunnel times. I love each of you and know without any doubt God will keep you strong until the end and give you wisdom.

How can you write a book without a great editor and publisher? Linda Ewing has been my editing savior over multiple books. She takes my incorrect sentence structure and poorly placed words and makes them come alive in perfect harmony. She was the first to compliment me on this book as she shared how it ministered to her personally during the editing process.

My publisher, Jean Thayer, has assisted on each of my books. She demonstrates remarkable precision in handling the details required for publishing. Jean also shared how the book ministered to her as she has found herself in some tunnels. Jean, thank you for your support.

Ryan —

I PRAY THE WORDS IN
THIS BOOK will MINISTER
TO YOU AS YOU TRAVEL
DOWN THE TRACKS OF
LIFE.

# 1

# HOPE IN THE TUNNELS

## How to get a GRIP

*"I pray that your hearts will be flooded with light so that you can understand the **confident hope** he has given to those he called—his holy people who are his rich and glorious inheritance."* (Ephesians 1:18)

Welcome aboard the train of life. Mile after mile you will run down the tracks in sunshine and happiness and then **bingo!** A dark tunnel will appear. Sometimes you see the tunnel coming, but many times you are in it before you know it.

Life runs along smoothly, and then we abruptly find ourselves in a tunnel of **hopelessness**. Many of you reading this book are in the tunnel of financial despair, health challenges, marriages that are beginning to erode, relationships that are rattling your emotional soul, children who have chosen to follow the world of drugs and alcohol, or the ultimate shot of **hopelessness**—losing a mate, child, or parent to death.

In my own life, I have gone through multiple tunnels, each time having that terrible four-letter word attack my spirit—**fear!** Waiting for a doctor's report on my wife's biopsy, standing and watching my equipment and fixtures being auctioned off in a collapsing company, having nothing to share with my kids at Christmas, seeing family relationships turn sour to mention only a few. The tunnel of **hopelessness** will make your nerves tingle from the base of your neck to the top of your head as you begin sweating in fear. Hopelessness is like a giant syringe in your brain, sucking out every live cell and making you totally lifeless.

Several months ago, I was sitting in my Bible-believing church. Each Sunday we are given the opportunity to take communion. My wife and I were sitting halfway back in the auditorium, the lights were turned down, and the sacraments were on a table in front of us. As the line of people passed the communion table, they appeared to be silhouettes, the outline of their bodies bouncing off the lighted stage behind them.

I thought to myself, Lord there are so many people with pain, seeking direction Sunday after Sunday, **hoping** that today's message from the pastor will be the tourniquet they can wrap around the bleeding of their spirits.

Each person is searching for the answer—how to regain the hope they once had. Each Sunday they come like desert camels seeking water, the water of hope.

I want to share this book with all who are searching for the path back to **hope**—not just hope but **confident hope.** For the new Christ-follower, this will be fresh information, an exciting trip, and for those who have been Christ-followers for years, if you've heard it before, hopefully it will confirm your own faith.

> *"I pray that your hearts will be flooded with light so that you can understand the **confident hope** he has given to those he called—his holy people who are his rich and glorious inheritance." (Eph. 1-18)*

This book is written for those who are in the tunnel — those who feel that crawling skin of nerves as they work to resolve a challenge in life. I must begin by saying that many of the words I am writing will not be understood if you have not accepted Jesus as your Lord and Savior.

> *But people who aren't spiritual [who don't know Christ] can't receive these truths [the Word] from God's Spirit. It all sounds foolish to them and they can't understand it, for only those who are spiritual [who accept Christ] can understand what the Spirit means. (I Cor. 2:14)*

The Word of God is clear that a person who has not asked Christ to take control of their life will not understand the words of the Bible. So let's not wait until the end of this book to become a member of God's Kingdom.

I have been labeled a "Type A" personality, one who wants answers now (you know the person who hates people who drive slow in the fast lane and who stands by an elevator and keeps pushing the elevator button even though the arrow light is on because he believes the elevator will come more quickly). In addition, I am a little ADD and love double shots of espresso, which really keeps me moving. Recently at a speaking engagement, a speech pathologist was sitting in the front row and afterward informed me that I speak 267 words a minute. I share this bit of news to help you understand why I believe in getting to the point quickly. So let's get down to business; I want to begin this book where most authors end, sharing the gospel of Jesus.

You see, a lost person cannot understand the things that are spiritual, and I have some great spiritual light to shine in this book. So if you have never asked Christ into your life, now is the time. Simply repeat these words from your heart: "Lord Jesus, come into my life; make me the person you want me to be. Fill my soul with your Spirit and lead me from this day forward with your wisdom. Thank you, Lord, for entering my life and taking control."

Well, that's it! I am confident you will not have any fireworks going off in your head, no explosions in the ears, no roar of thunder from heaven, just a simple confirmation in your heart that all is well.

I am excited you have joined me and millions around the world who have made the same decision. God's Word shares that we are to repent and turn in a new direction. If you have sincerely asked Christ into your life, you will turn and begin a new direction. How refreshing it is.

Before the recent passing of my dear friend and mentor, Zig Ziglar, I was at the headquarters of his business, The Zig Ziglar Corporation in Dallas, Texas. They had asked me to share at their Monday morning devotional—quite an honor. After the devotional, Zig leaned over to me in the board room and said this: "Bobby, I have figured this whole thing out." I said, "Really Zig, what is it?" His response—"We are not getting out of here alive."

Folks, as simple as it sounds, we shall all face death, and each of us will spend eternity somewhere.

So asking Christ to take control of your life has just finalized where you will be spending eternity with your friends Bob Goshen, Zig Ziglar, and millions of others.

If you have just asked Christ into your life, drop me a note at bob@bobgoshen.com and let me know so I can send you a personal welcome to the kingdom! If you have previously asked Christ to take control of your life, then **super good**, we will enjoy being together over the next few days as you read this book. If you did not accept this invitation and are not a Christ-follower, then hang in here, and I am confident you will gain some knowledge you can use. I am confident God will shed some light, for His Word is sharper than a two-edged sword.

Let's start with a brutally realistic truth. Life is more like a salvage operation than a day at the beach. Most of us will spend more time in our lives recuperating rather than rejoicing. Ouch! Bob, do you have to be so blunt? Especially at the beginning of the book? I mean come on, where are the warm and fuzzy words confirming that God will give me the easy life and all will be riches and fame from the day I become a Christ-follower? Bob, even last week my pastor said I could have anything I ask, and if I just have faith all things will come together, and I will be blessed.

Well, here is the truth. God does love you and that will never change; you will never be able to separate from His love. However, when you follow the disciples and the Apostle Paul's life, it is obvious they were constantly regrouping.

So let's begin by being on the offense. Yes, let's stop running from what is happening in our lives and ask how we can take anything in life head on and overcome.

If you are going to function as an effective Christ-follower, then start today by eliminating these words: "I can't believe this has happened," or "I can't believe this has happened to **me**," or "**Why** would this happen to me?" As a non-board certified psychologist, let me say "Get out of the river of denial." It **is** happening to you, or as I tell my kids, "It is what it is."

Your current tunnel is happening in your life for a godly reason. You say, "Godly reason? Are you saying God knows about my problems? If He knows about them, why is He letting this happen?" My friend, He not only knows your problems but also makes it clear you need to accept them joyfully.

Get this picture: let's say your brother is Jesus, and you decide to write a short book on principles. If you were the brother of Jesus, how would you start your book?

I would most likely begin by saying, "This letter is from Bob, the stud brother of Jesus," or maybe "Hey folks, I am the number one bro of Jesus. So you need to hear me out."

Go to the book of James and read chapter one, which **was** written by the brother of Jesus. Relationship means everything, so let's see what His brother thought was so important.

> This letter is from James, **a slave of God and of the Lord Jesus Christ** - *"Dear brothers and sisters* [that would be us], *when troubles come your way, consider it an opportunity for great joy."* (James 1:1-2)

Great joy! Are you kidding me, Bob? What are you talking about—great joy? Can't you understand my pain? Let's read on:

> *"For you know that when your faith is tested, your endurance has a chance to grow. So let it grow, for when your endurance is fully developed, you will be perfect and complete, needing nothing."* (James 1:3-4)

Okay, let's see if I get this. When I am in that tunnel, I am to look for opportunity for great joy, for the ride is to test my faith and give me endurance. Wow! I know that is a lot to digest. But let me tell you how to get from downhearted to delighted, from defeated to triumphant, from destroyed to victorious.

### Get a GRIP

If you will get a **GRIP** on what is happening, you will make it through the tunnels, the challenges, and grow while you are experiencing them. I often use an acronym to explain just how to "get a grip." The "**G**" stands for **GOD is in control**. Period!

If you can always come back to this most basic truth, that God is in control during all of your challenges and that God is sovereign, your time of trial can become a time of triumph. You see, God is not surprised by our challenges. God saw them before they happened, and because of this we can rest assured He will see us through them!

God is sovereign! Check out the definition: "A supreme ruler; possessing supreme or ultimate power; one that exercises supreme, permanent authority." Are you getting it? As an Aggie (pray for me) I would say "God does what God wants to do – period! That settles it!" God is supreme in my life and has authority over my life. Today that is a hard one to swallow, right?

Most everyone demands their rights. We have gay rights, equal rights, women's rights, worker's rights, children's rights, animal rights, civil rights, and environmental rights. So to say that God is in control immediately strips that "rights" issue out from under our feet.

So dig it! You are in a tunnel at this moment or perhaps headed for a tunnel. Relieve the tension immediately by saying "**God is in control.**"

I love Carrie Underwood for two reasons. She is from my home state, Oklahoma, and she sings country/western music. There are only two types of music I will listen to—country and western. Her first number one song that blew off the charts was *Jesus, Take the Wheel*.

Fact is, Jesus already had the wheel, the car, the driver, and control of the road conditions (have I stretched the old neo-cortex side of the brain yet?) Habakkuk (say that three times quickly) chapter 3 verse 19 claims:

> *The Sovereign Lord is my strength! [When you enter the tunnel, repeat those 6 words over and over]. He makes me as surefooted as a deer, [not an octopus on roller skates—but a deer] able to tread upon the heights.*

One more, Acts 4:24:

> *When they heard the report, all the believers lifted their voices together in prayer to God: "O* **Sovereign Lord***, Creator of Heaven and earth, the sea, and everything in them. . . ."*

Check it out, a sovereign God created heaven, the earth, and the sea, but don't overlook **and everything in them**. Hello! Guess who the **everything in them** might be? You got it! **You!** We are the "everything" in them.

I think it might be safe to say that the God who created heaven and the earth and you is going with you through this tunnel. You will recognize His presence if you will look up and not down.

So the "G" in **GRIP** stands for **God is in control.** Period! That settles it!

The "R" in my acronym is for **REJOICE during the challenge**. Man you are nuts, Bob. I am in the biggest battle of my life, and you are saying rejoice. You are an insane Aggie! Settle down; no need to get the old blood pressure moving in a northward direction.

> *Then I will **rejoice** in the LORD. I will be glad because he rescues me. (Psalm 35:9)*

> *Whatever happens, my dear brothers and sisters, [again, that would be us] **rejoice** in the Lord. (Phil.3: 1)*

> *We can **rejoice,** too, when we run into problems and trials, for we know that they help us develop endurance. (Romans 5:3)*

Whoa! Endurance. We'll deal with that dirty word later. Let's be clear; the Word of God is not asking you to rejoice **for** your problems but rather to rejoice **in** your problems.

I have discovered that major stress is the number one challenge we face during all the negative events in our lives. Major stress can trigger all sorts of additional issues from cancer to strokes to something as simple as elevated blood pressure. The stress keeps our "nerves on edge" and pulls our immune system to the basement. Rejoicing disengages that element of the challenge and allows God to teach us and open up our minds to His wisdom during these times of trauma. His Word is clear:

> *Always be joyful. Never stop praying. Be thankful in all circumstances, for this is God's will for you who belong to Christ Jesus. (1 Thessalonians 5:16-18)*

Read carefully; it does not say be thankful **for** the circumstance but rather be thankful **in** all circumstances. My wife, Kay, and I often pray when we are in the tunnel: "Lord, we remain joyful in you, and we are thankful for what we will learn during this circumstance." Tough bullet to take, but much better than anxiety and worry.

By thanking God and giving Him the challenge, we allow our mental capacity to remain open to His direction. So number one, **God is in control**, and number two, **rejoice during the challenge**—the times of trouble and trial.

What a sandwich, huh? God and rejoicing with troubles and pain in-between.

Bob, can we just call this chapter **GR** and stop now instead of finishing the **GRIP**? Not sure if I can handle the **IP** portion.

Sure you can, for the hardest part is over— learning how to surrender our pride and rights and then rejoicing in our God on high is the biggest challenge to our spirit.

Next, **INITIATE your faith**. Here we have this negative challenge that has entered our life—financial, marital, parental, or other such challenges, and we are now in the middle of our tunnel or just entering it.

We have surrendered to the fact that God is in total control; we are rejoicing to eliminate the stress and telling God He can work through us during this trial. It is now time to put our **faith** to work.

> **Faith** is the confidence that what we hope for will actually happen; it gives us assurance about things we cannot see. (Hebrews 11:1)

I enjoy my wife's interpretation: "Faith is believing something is so when it is not so, so it can be so." Wow! Simple, but pretty much says it all.

These are not just clever words. Let me tell how they applied to a marriage that was unholy and rotten for the first seven years a couple spent together.

The husband was full of foul language, did not believe in God, put his wife down with his words, and put her down for her belief in God.

He made his positions clear with local pastors and told them what he thought of the physical church to the point that the neighborhood pastors knew never to visit her home.

She had one Doctor of Theology from a large church tell her he had never seen a man as reprobate as her husband ever come to God. How would you like to hear that about your husband? After a while, she stopped praying for her husband's salvation and began praying to God to be sure she was in alignment and her heart was pure.

God instructed her to begin believing her husband was saved, even when he was not saved, so he could be saved. She found a scripture that quickened her heart:

> *"In the same way, you wives must accept the authority of your husbands. Then, even if some refuse to obey the Good News, your godly lives will speak to them without any words. They will be won over by observing your pure and reverent lives." (1 Peter 3:1-2)*

Some of you ladies are jumping out of your Nordstrom sandals saying she was crazy! Faith is one thing; being stupid is something totally different. Guess what? Her actions of faith and prayer were answered. I was actually there the day this husband broke down and accepted Christ as his Lord and Savior, for I am that husband. Thank God for a woman of focused faith; her submission led to my admission to heaven!

Faith is key when you are in the tunnel of despair and pain. You see, **confident hope** depends on total faith. Confident hope is saying "I expect" something to happen in order to complete God's will in my life—not my will, but His will be done. Listen to the words of Jesus:

> *"My father! If it is possible, let this cup of suffering be taken away from me. Yet I want your will to be done, not mine." (Matthew 26:39b)*

So often in my life I have tried to work my will instead of the will of God. Each time the outcome has been less than pretty. Faith says "Lord I am in this tunnel; You are sovereign, and You are in control. I will rejoice and focus my faith muscle to achieve Your will."

> *Jonathan went to find David and encouraged him to stay strong in his **faith** in God. (1 Samuel 23:16)*

I am asking you to remain strong in your faith as you go through your current tunnel. I know it is very difficult at this time. I know you are weak, and anxiety has you in a constant state of fear. I can feel your stomach turn over each time you swallow, and I feel your heart race.

It hurts. The tunnel is working to defeat you, but ask God for a supernatural shot of faith during this time of fear. It is faith that makes it possible to remain confident in hope, taking the pain from the hurt. Listen:

> *"Whatever happens, my dear brothers and sisters, rejoice in the Lord. I never get tired of telling you these things, and I do it to safeguard your **faith**." (Phil: 3:1)*

Do you realize it is impossible to please God without faith? Bob, things are bad enough. Please don't put me on a guilt trip. Faith is the number one measurement to determine how we are pleasing God.

> *"And it is impossible to please God without **faith**. Anyone who wants to come to him must believe that God exists and that he rewards those who sincerely seek him." (Hebrews 11:6)*

Not funny, Bob. Now I am responsible for that bit of information. Ugh! My dear friends, when you find yourself in that tunnel or perhaps about to enter that tunnel, seek Him, and put your best "faith step" forward.

Have the faith to see this challenge through knowing it might not be pretty but remembering that God is in control!

Bob, please slow down! You are stretching my thinking more than Fruit of the Looms® on a 300 pound NFL lineman. So let's see if I understand it so far. We must learn to stop making excuses by saying, "I can't believe this is happening to me." This kind of thinking automatically sets our minds in a position of pity instead of possibility.

In other words, Bob, you are saying we should get ready to take on a life of recovery with our guns loaded to immediately jump in and get a grip. Correct? So, we have the **GRI**. What's the **P**? Preparing our last will and testament?

Good thing to do, but the final letter is **P** for **PRAYER.** Here you are in this tunnel of obvious tragedy with relationships, drugs, alcohol, death, or whatever, so what do you pray? I have found in my own life when I took the self-centered way, I began praying for God to take away the pain, release me from the fear, pull me out of the financial pit, or just make the problem go away. Amazing how through what I call the "name it and claim it" mentality, we feel we can move God around like a pinball, sort of a vending machine God.

Put my dollar in and pull the handle on the solution I want. Funny, huh? We say God is sovereign, but we think we have the capacity to move Him where we want so He will make the decisions we want.

Several years ago I was invited to speak at a Christian Businessmen's luncheon. My message was short and pointed, speaking about how we go through life thinking that we call all the shots. Even as believers, we think we have a special hall pass to do whatever we feel like doing. If we have financial challenges, we pray something like this: "Lord, you know I am late on my car payment. You know the exact amount, and God I now expect that amount to appear in my bank account. Amen."

There was a time in my life when I found myself praying for things—more money, more time, more, more, more, more. Fortunately the Lord figuratively slapped me across the face and showed me a verse that **jumped out**.

> *"Tune your ears to wisdom, and concentrate on understanding. Cry out for insight, and ask for understanding. Search for them as you would for silver; seek them like hidden treasures. . . . .*
>
> *For the LORD grants wisdom!" (Proverbs 2:2-4, 6)*
>
> *"If you need wisdom, ask our generous God, and he will give it to you. He will not rebuke you for asking." (James 1:5)*

You see, we spend so much time asking God for **things** rather than asking God for His **wisdom**.

How about this: "Lord, my prayer is simple; give me wisdom as I enter this tunnel. Show me what you want me to learn and how this tunnel can prepare me to better serve you here on earth." The Word of God is clear when it says that wisdom is more valuable than silver and gold, but we continue to pray for the silver and gold and not for wisdom.

So no more excuses, nope not anymore. Don't run to your pastor with this "I can't believe it" attitude. **Get ready for your next tunnel with confident hope because you know how to get a GRIP.**

# 2

# PATIENT IN TROUBLE

*"I pray that your hearts will be flooded with light so that you can understand the **confident hope** he has given to those he called — his holy people who are his rich and glorious inheritance."*
*(Ephesians 1:18)*

My time in the military was spent in naval intelligence. I would actually intercept communication from the Russians, break it down, and send it to Washington, DC. That's right; "break it down" like a good hip-hop song. When I completed my service, I had this benefit called the GI Bill, and I decided to apply this advantage to getting my private pilot's license.

My wife is indebted to me as I improved her prayer life tremendously each time she would fly with me. I have really added value to her spiritual growth.

Soon after I received my license, I decided to impress my 12-year-old son and take him up on a short trip to Arkansas.

As we left our home airport in Tulsa, I began to gain altitude only to see heavy storm clouds in front of me. Being a responsible pilot, I did what any ignorant pilot would do. I began to climb higher to get over the clouds. We were climbing and climbing and climbing, and all of a sudden I could climb no higher. I was in the clouds (without an instrument rating) and hearing my engine go cough-cough-cough! The propeller stopped — for those of you who are not astute in the realm of aviation, you need to recognize that as a "sign." I heard my young son say, "Daddy, I can't breathe." And a scientific point: there is an altitude that once exceeded leaves no more air in your cockpit. Seeing my son's blue lips and his gray face was a good indicator of this scientific fact.

I looked to the right to see this little hole in the clouds, and I put my plane in a 45° bank and started to spiral through this little hole in the clouds.

My son asked the question of all questions: "Daddy, are we going to be alright?"

With all the confidence I could muster and in a voice that sounded like "Tiny Tim's" (for those of you who did not know Tiny Tim, let's just say my voice was 24 octaves higher than normal) I said, "Sure Robby, all is well."

When he asked, "Daddy, why are you sweating?" I answered in my most confident voice, "Just releasing a few toxins my son!" Romans 12:12 came alive, for once I saw that hole in the clouds I began rejoicing and working to remain **patient in my time of trouble** while I kept on praying.

So it is as we enter these various tunnels during our lifetime. We must keep on praying in times of trouble, asking for God's wisdom, working constantly to **remain patient** while we pass through the tunnels.

Yes, we did survive, and the next day I went back to school to get my instrument and multi-engine ratings, and now I am prepared to enter the clouds. In the same way, I have found I continue to return to the ultimate textbook (the Word of God) to get equipped to enter my next tunnel.

## When Challenges Come

It is not a question of whether tunnels will confront us. The question is how we respond as we enter the tunnel. I have shared how to immediately get a **GRIP,** but let's back it up with a unique story and passage.

Kay and I have been through many tunnels in our life together, but I remember one time when we simply had no answers. We used our **GRIP** principle, but we still needed more. Isn't it wonderful when you are open for wisdom and you call upon the Lord how He answers you in His handbook for life? So, there we sat, sort of paralyzed, understanding God's will but hungry for an answer when **bingo!** God showed us a passage in Scripture.

This passage immediately ministered to us, and I believe it will minister to you as well when you enter one of those tunnels of challenge.

Jehoshaphat was getting ready to go into a major tunnel, the tunnel of war. (2 Chronicles 20:1-21)

> *After this, the armies of the Moabites, Ammonites, and some of the Meunites declared war on Jehoshaphat.* [Weird names, huh? I would want to go fight if someone named my tribe the Meunites. I wonder if this is where we got the statement Holy Jehoshaphat.] *Some messengers came and told Jehoshaphat, "A vast army from Edom is marching against you from beyond the Dead*

*Sea. They are already at Hazazon-tamar."*
[This was another name for En-gedi.]
*Jehoshaphat was terrified by this news and begged the LORD for guidance. He also ordered everyone in Judah to begin fasting. So people from all the towns of Judah came to Jerusalem to seek the LORD's help. Jehoshaphat stood before the community of Judah and Jerusalem in front of the new courtyard at the Temple of the LORD. He prayed, "O LORD, God of our ancestors, you alone are the God who is in heaven. You are ruler of all the kingdoms of the earth. You are powerful and mighty; no one can stand against you! O our God, did you not drive out those who lived in this land when your people Israel arrived? And did you not give this land forever to the descendants of your friend Abraham? Your people settled here and built this Temple to honor your name. They said, 'Whenever we are faced with any calamity such as war, plague, or famine, we can come to stand in your presence before this Temple where your name is honored. We can cry out to you to save us, and you will hear us and rescue us.' And now see what the armies of Ammon, Moab and Mount Seir are doing. You would not let our ancestors invade those nations when Israel left Egypt, so they went around them and did not destroy them. Now see how they reward us! For they have come to throw us out of your land,*

23

*which you gave us as an inheritance. O our God, won't you stop them? We are powerless against this mighty army that is about to attack us. We do not know what to do, but we are looking to you for help."*

OK, here is the bottom line: Jehoshaphat is about to get slaughtered by multiple armies. You say Bob, *"That is good history, but what does this have to do with me?"* So glad you asked. Again, let's break it down!

Jehoshaphat was **terrified** by the news. How about you as you enter your tunnel? Ever been **terrified**? So what did he do? Jehoshaphat "begged the Lord for guidance." He didn't ask the Lord; he didn't suggest to the Lord, no he **begged** the Lord for what? Not escape but rather for **guidance**.

Jehoshaphat prayed: *"O LORD, God of our ancestors, you alone are the God who is in heaven. You are ruler of all the kingdoms of the earth."* He acknowledged God's sovereignty—that God was in total control then as He had always been. *"You are ruler of all the kingdoms of the earth. You are powerful and mighty; no one can stand against you!"*

When you enter the tunnel, the Lord gives you permission to cry out to him. The Israelites said, *"We can cry out to you to save us, and you will hear us and rescue us."* They **pleaded** *"O our God, won't you stop them?* [Lord won't you stop what is happening in my life at this moment?] *We are powerless against this mighty army that is about to attack us. We do not know what to do, but we are looking to you for help."*

24

Wow! Double wow! Summary: You will be **terrified** at times. When those times come, don't suggest that God might want to get involved in your situation—**beg** Him for guidance. Then acknowledge to God that He is in control, He is sovereign. Get alone and **cry out**, really cry out to God knowing He will hear you. When we acknowledge His control and His sovereignty, we can confidently cry out to God knowing He will hear. Say to Him as the Israelites said: **"We do not know what to do, but we are looking to you for help."** This was an amazing example to my wife and me during a critical time. We believe it was God's "step-by-step" instruction on what we were to do.

Now let's examine how God responded to the people and to King Jehoshaphat. God spoke to them through a man named Jahaziel who just happened to be standing nearby:

> *"Listen all of you people of Judah and Jerusalem! Listen, King Jehoshaphat! This is what the LORD says: Do not be afraid! Don't be discouraged by this mighty army, for the battle is not yours, but God's."*

What is the mighty army marching against you at this time? Divorce, disease, financial difficulties, broken relationships?

It matters not. God would say to you, *"Don't be afraid! Kill the fear. Don't be discouraged by your tunnel. Lift your head up to Me, not down to sorrow. This is not your battle; it is Mine!"* God says it clearly: *"This is My battle, have faith in My ability.*

*If I can create the heavens and the earth and if I can divide the Red Sea, I can handle your situation."*

The next day, as King Jehoshaphat was leading his army to the appointed battleground, he stopped and told his people:

> *"Believe in the LORD your God, and you will be able to stand firm. Believe in his prophets, and you will succeed."*

Now, sit down and hold on because the Lord is going to stretch your faith with this next little bit of history.

> *After consulting the people, the king appointed singers to walk ahead of the army, singing to the LORD and praising him for his holy splendor. This is what they sang:* [Can you imagine this? Here is a group of people who have been instructed to march toward horrific armies unarmed and singing.] ***"Give thanks to the LORD; His faithful love endures forever!"***

**Faith?** That's what I'm talking about! God simply says, *"Forget about fighting. Just march over the mountain and the battle will be won!"* You are currently in your own battle (tunnel). God tells you to stand up, march, and sing these words: *"Give thanks to the Lord; His faithful love endures forever!"* Notice the exclamation point; it's very important. This is **not** a suggestion; it is a **command**. A side note here: Kay and I put these words up on our refrigerator, rear view mirror, on all of our mirrors, and on the window of our back door, and I might suggest you do the same. Commit this to your heart, never stop marching forward in **faith** and singing the words God commanded.

Read 2 Chronicles 20:24, and you will see God's amazing hand going in front of the people to win the battle. You see my friends, the tunnels will come, but God is ready to take us through the tunnel to His light.

> *We can make our plans, but the LORD determines our steps. (Proverbs 16:9)*

Just like the homework they gave us in school, this is now your homework for this week. Each time tunnels seem to be coming, run back to get a **GRIP**, but while running repeat these words:

> **Give thanks to the LORD; His faithful love endures forever!**

At this very moment I want you to repeat these words 10 times and feel your fear move to faith! Sense the same peace that the people of Judah felt when they marched out in faith toward their tunnel.

Later in the passage, we learn what happened when the battle was over, when Jehoshaphat emerged from his tunnel:

> *So Jehoshaphat's kingdom was at peace, for his God had given him rest on every side. (2Chronicles 20:30)*

Kay and I have been in many tunnels, but each time as we held on to God's truth we came out surrounded by His rest on every side.

So whether you are in the clouds as I was with my son, totally unprepared and totally terrified, or in your current tunnel of fear, God has given you the formula for being patient in trouble as you look for the light and peace He promises.

# 3

# CONFIDENT IN CHRIST

*"I pray that God, the source of hope, will fill you completely with joy and peace because you trust in him. Then you will overflow with **confident hope** through the power of the Holy Spirit."* (Romans 15:13)

Several years ago, an outstanding book was introduced entitled *The Purpose Driven Life* by Rick Warren. Everyone was astonished to see how this book was received both in and out of the Christian community. To me, it was the first wakeup call on how many people are searching for direction in life.

So many today are searching for the real truth, yet at the same time so many people are living without confidence.

When I speak on leadership to corporations, I begin by sitting down with the CEO and asking him to tell me his biggest challenge. Without hesitation, more often than not I hear "I have more tasks than I have leaders to lead the tasks." The corporation may be overrun with titled people, but lean when it comes to people who can step up with confidence and get a job done. I recently shared a leadership presentation with a group of MBA's and told them, "Your diploma is great, but it does just one thing. It gets you across the threshold."

In my recent book, *The Power of Layered Leadership,* I talk about confidence. The thesis of the book is **when you get the person right, everything works**: your marriage, your job, relationships with others, and more.

As I travel around the world sharing leadership skills, I have discovered that people have so much doubt in their personal ability that they have very little joy and peace. Many reading this book have experienced a disastrous past. Perhaps as a child you were told you would never make it in life, or maybe you have a mate who has put you down with his/her sharp words of destruction.

Some of you have done terrible things to your body through the use of drugs and alcohol, and of course there are many who have been mentally or sexually abused. Until you meet these past experiences head-on and defeat them, your lack of confidence will make it difficult for you to move through or escape the tunnel.

Well, this chapter of my book has but one purpose, and that is to allow you the opportunity to drop the past, to focus on the future, and to begin believing God for your results. I want you to realize that God has a plan and a purpose for your life. Yes, you may be in that tunnel or approaching one, but if you can begin to believe that God knows where you are, then your future becomes much brighter.

You are just like those folks of Judah I told you about. Even though you feel totally defeated, God made it clear to them and He makes it clear to you that you are special and that He will walk before you to accomplish His purpose.

I tell a story in *The Power of Layered Leadership* about a young man that I coached in high school football. He was a great athlete, he had the size, the ability, the mental awareness, and he had what we would say is the "total package."

This young man's challenge was that each time he missed a tackle he would come back to the huddle in disgust and anger, talking about his failure. "I should have done this, I could have done that, and I can't believe I missed the tackle." He would spend so much time and energy reliving the last play that he was never really set for the next play. So it is in life. Some of you are allowing yourselves to live in the past, saying "I can't believe this happened," or "I wish I would have done it differently," or "It just wasn't right to be treated the way I was treated." Let's face it, we were all born into sin, each and every one of us have something in our past that we could dwell on forever.

Sadly, many do dwell there, and many do not believe they now deserve a new beginning or that there is a way out of their current tunnel. They need to "break the rearview mirror" that keeps them looking back.

Let's examine some information I received within the first few weeks after I asked Christ to come into my life. You see, I was 31 years of age when I asked Christ to take control of my life, to make me the husband and father that I wanted to become. My first 31 years on this planet are not years I am proud of.

My father was an alcoholic, and even though I was an above average athlete and was successful in three sports, he never attended any of my games. He was abusive with his language, continually putting people down, and focused entirely on what he wanted. We were not people of means when I was growing up. The first home we rented when I was young was 400 square feet. I tell folks we not only had bunk beds, we had bunk chairs.

I do have to admit the bathroom was much more convenient than many today. It was one small room that didn't have a door. It had a curtain you pulled; I am pretty sure it was a bed sheet. Once inside, you would sit down on the toilet with the sink immediately in front of you, which made it possible to "use the facilities" and brush your teeth at the same time.

My high school football coach would not recommend me to a college because he said I did not have the proper attitude and I would never make it. I met Kay when she was 15 and I was 17. Her mother immediately let me know my value by telling me never to see Kay. Needless to say, by the time I got out of high school I did not think too highly of myself.

As time passed, Kay and I did get married, I did go back to college and play football, and I did get a bigger bathroom. Hallelujah! But I still did not see myself as being special until I became aware of a chapter in the Bible, Psalm 139. Listen to these words, my friends; read them slowly and meditate on them:

> *"O LORD, you have examined my heart and know everything about me. You know when I sit down or stand up. You know my thoughts*

*even when I'm far away. You see me when I travel and when I rest at home. You know everything I do. You know what I am going to say even before I say it, LORD. You go before me and follow me [is that cool or what, before us and behind us]. You place your hand of blessing on my head. Such knowledge is too wonderful for me, too great for me to understand! [I still do not understand, but I do believe it.] I can never escape from your Spirit! I can never get away from your presence! If I go up to heaven, you are there; if I go down to the grave, you are there. If I ride the wings of the morning, if I dwell by the farthest oceans, even there your hand will guide me, and your strength will support me. I could ask the darkness to hide me and the light around me to become night—but even in darkness I cannot hide from you. To you the night shines as bright as day. Darkness and light are the same to you."*

**Wowzer!** Are you getting it? Ponder what I just shared. God knew and was around when I had a father that was an alcoholic, a mother-in-law who did not see my greatness, and a coach who put me down. He was there and He knew what was happening.

If you think what I have shared is cool, you had better put on your seat belt because the next few verses are the ones that brought me out of the mental captivity of worthlessness to becoming a person of immense value destined for greatness. Here we go! (I am going to write this in bold type so you will be sure to see it!)

> *"You made all the delicate, inner parts of my body and knit me together in my mother's womb.* [Check it out. Not after you and I were born, but he designed us in our mother's womb. As Randy Jackson would say on American Idol, "Yo." But now catch this.] *Thank you for making me so wonderfully complex! Your workmanship is marvelous—how well I know it. You watched me as I was being formed in utter seclusion, as I was woven together in the dark of the womb. You saw me before I was born."*

He was making you into a great creation in your mother's womb. Now hang on; we are headed for the final blast of the fireworks show.

> *"Every day of my life was recorded in your book. Every moment was laid out before a single day had passed."*

Excuse me while I go outside running and shouting, **"Are you getting this?"** Let's break it down in Goshenology: before you were born, God had a plan and a purpose for your life. Everything you and I have experienced might have surprised us, but God was never surprised. God knew and knows about everything that has happened and will happen to us. We can confidently trust that His intent is for our good, to grow us, and often to enable us to take any pain we experience and share with others who are having the same sufferings. **Glory!** You see it matters **not** what man says to you or does to you; who cares? The one who created you has the ultimate plan for you.

So today, at this very moment, I want you to drop the past—all the pain, all the hate, envy, jealousy, on and on and on and simply say, "**I have been wonderfully and fearfully made** by a God who knows what He is doing. In all that has happened to me, man may have meant it for harm, but God makes it for good."

Here is a little homework exercise (I never did like homework as evident by my college grades). I want you to take a piece of paper from a yellow pad or notepad or PostIt. It doesn't matter what you find.

I want you to write down everything in your past that has held you back—every pain, every torment, every negative thought, and every negative action of a friend or family member, every excuse you have been using for surviving instead of thriving. Write it down, and then go into your bathroom (hopefully bigger than my first bathroom). Tear up the paper; rip the past into little pieces, all the experiences that have been holding you back. Drop all the pieces into the toilet and do the **giant flush**! As the bits of paper are swirling into the sewer, take out your phone, shoot a picture, and send it to bob@bobgoshen.com.

Attach a note stating that you are now set free and ready to listen to God instead of your relative or the negative friends who seem to have all the answers on why you are losing in life.

I love Joel Osteen and have had the opportunity to visit his church on many occasions. He made me laugh when he once said, "There are some people you are going to need to love from a distance." Amen, Mr. Joel. Amen.

> It is senseless to pay tuition to educate a fool, since he has no heart for learning. (Proverbs 17:16)

Some of you need to stay clear of the fools in life who wish to hold you in the world of mediocrity and life's "ol' poor me" sewer. When you understand to stay far from these folks, you will move through life with pleasure. Yes, my friend, when you accept the belief that God is in control of your life, your life changes dramatically.

> We may throw the dice, but the LORD determines how they fall. (Proverbs 16:33)

> We can make our plans, but the LORD determines our steps. (Proverbs 16:9)

We can live in the confidence of God's control. He knows our thoughts and our actions. He saw us in our mother's womb and through all of our past tunnels and is ready to let us know He can carry us through any future tunnels. Makes you want to run and shout too, right? As my dear friend and mentor, Lou Holtz, says at the close of his presentations: "I know not what tomorrow holds, but I do know who holds tomorrow." Once again, amen Brother Lou!

My friends, when you can confidently put your arms around the fact that God has a purpose and plan for your life and He is bringing you to maturity in this plan, life does not necessarily become easier, but it does become more understandable seeing God's sovereign and divine hand at work. I've never seen hindsight bring anyone closer to God, and He will never give you more than you can handle.

The Lord has put many godly men in my life to take me to the next level of spiritual growth, and one such gentleman was John Blanchard. John is an evangelist from England who has been given the gift of bringing life to the Word of God. I shall never forget the day John was sharing a message, and he began by talking about ships in the harbor in England. He said that on the side of the ship there is a line drawn from bow to stern; this line is known as a "Plimsoll line." The Plimsoll line is there for those who are loading the ship. They monitor it to ensure they do not load the ship to the point that the Plimsoll line is no longer visible. In essence, it is a mark on the boat to ensure the ship is not overloaded.

John uses this illustration to demonstrate that God has a Plimsoll line on every individual. He will never load us beyond our ability to handle the challenge, and God will always offer us a way of escape. We should never believe our temptations are unique, never ever believe we will get through life without challenges, but always rest assured that God has a plan.

> *If you think you are standing strong, be careful not to fall. The temptations in your life are no different from what others experience. And God is faithful. He will not allow the temptation to be more than you can stand. When you are tempted, he will show you a way out so that you can endure. (I Corinthians 10:12-13)*

When you find yourself at the next tunnel's entry, know that God sees the challenge; He will not give you more than you can handle, and He will always give you the grace to endure. (Can I get an amen, brothers and sisters?)

> *Trust in the LORD with all your heart; do not depend on your own understanding. Seek his will in all you do, and he will show you which path to take. (Proverbs 3:5)*

Do not depend on your own understanding. Seek His will, not your will, and He promises to show you the correct path. Surrender your rights and God will give them back to you as privileges. Kill your pride and become humble before the Lord.

> *Pride leads to disgrace, but with humility comes wisdom. (Proverbs 11:2)*

Man I am so excited about that verse I am ready to take an offering.

My biggest wakeup call came when I found that my life has nothing to do with my plans but rather with God's plans for using me. He gave us the gift of inheritance, to be with him eternally, and now he is working His plan in my life and your life.

> *Furthermore, because we are united with Christ, we have received an inheritance from God, for* **He chose us in advance, and He makes everything work out according to his plan.** *(Ephesians 1:11)*

### Joy and Peace

I began chapter three with Romans 15:13, *"I pray that God, the source of hope, will fill you completely with joy and peace...."*

When you are in the tunnel or headed for the tunnel, it is difficult to find those two words in your spirit. Our spirits normally scream **sadness** and **fear.** But yet I have found that the word "joy" appears in the Bible 333 times, and the word "peace" appears 362 times.

It is my belief that God wants us to know about these two words and learn how to incorporate them in our "tunnel time" (sounds cool—tunnel time). Do you think I need to change the title of the book to *Tunnel Time*? Would make a great cartoon show; ladies and gentlemen, boys and girls, welcome to *Tunnel Time!*

Joy! Remember James 1:2? *"Dear brothers and sisters, when troubles come your way, consider it an opportunity for great joy."*

Again, take note. James says **when** troubles come our way, not if troubles **should** or **might** come our way. He makes it clear that we will have tunnel time. When headed for the tunnel, James says to consider it an opportunity for great joy. Now that just doesn't seem right to me. It is like saying, "OK, you are getting ready to crash so look at it as an opportunity to enjoy the scenery!" Try to share that with the average person who is not familiar with the Word of God.

But you see when we are aware of God's vision and provision, we quickly begin to understand that the tunnel is meant to build us, not destroy us, while exalting our Savior. God cannot begin the calming process until we become joyful.

*For the LORD your God is living among you. He is a mighty savior. He will take delight in you with gladness. With his love, **he will calm all your fears.** He will rejoice over you with **joyful** songs. (Zephaniah 3:17)*

God reveals his Word to us more clearly in times of trouble, when we are in the tunnel rather than out of the tunnel. The tunnel times have normally been the times I find myself seeking the Word more and praying more fervently. I am confident everyone reading this book is not like me; you are most likely very diligent each day to spend hours in the Word of God reading and then praying. But I have to confess, when I am out of the tunnel there are times I find myself reading the Word but not "consuming" the Word.

However, when I am entering a tunnel or in the tunnel, my depth of prayer and reading become much more focused. I begin to experience the joy and peace we are talking about. I hate to admit that, but often it has taken a tunnel experience to get me back into "right standing" with the Lord. So when the tunnel comes, if I **run** to the Word of God and begin seeking His **will and wisdom,** I find immediate joy.

> *I have told you these things so that you will be*
> *filled with my **joy.** Yes, your **joy** will overflow!*
> *(John 15:11)*

Another way to say it: *"When I have told you these things which are in my Word, you will be filled with joy."* God has given us a stress reliever for when we are in the tunnel. We are to become joyful, not for what is happening but in spite of what is happening. His Word says:

> *So you have sorrow now, but I will see you*
> *again; then you will rejoice, and no one can rob*
> *you of that **joy.** (John 16:22)*

As we enter the tunnel, we can all say we enter with sorrow. But if we open up the Word of God, He will "reveal" His purpose, and we can begin experiencing His joy. When Kay and I look back over the tunnel times in our lives, when we felt we would never make it, we see that over time God restored our joy and ultimately showed us the why. In Romans we read:

> *For the Kingdom of God is not a matter of what we eat or drink, but of living a life of goodness and peace and **joy** in the Holy Spirit. (Romans 14:17)*

Kay and I have always found that the faster we can run back to the "foot of the cross" and acknowledge God's sovereignty, the quicker joy is released in our spirits.

> *So be truly glad. There is wonderful **joy** ahead, even though you have to endure many trials for a little while. (1 Peter 1:6)*

> *Instead, be very glad—for these trials make you partners with Christ in his suffering, so that you will have the wonderful **joy** of seeing his glory when it is revealed to all the world. (1 Peter 4:13)*

Yes, we will have trials, yes we will be in and out of tunnels, but God says keep the faith and your joy will be filled.

## Peace

When we are in that tunnel of fear, our peace and strength are based upon how fast we can get into the Word of Life. Many who are reading this book feel the clutches of fear and its accompanying discouragement and weakness.

There have been times in my life I just had no energy and no hope, the fear was overwhelming as my brain raced through all the possible scenarios to my trial.

> *"Don't be afraid," he said, "for you are very precious to God. **Peace!** Be encouraged! Be Strong!" As he spoke these words to me, I suddenly felt stronger and said to him, "Please speak to me, my lord, for you have strengthened me." (Daniel 10:19)*

Let the Lord speak to you. To experience peace, we must run to His Word. When these challenges occur, it seems like everything is totally out of order, nothing makes sense, and things seem so out of control and confusing, but listen:

> *For God is not a God of disorder but of **peace**, as in all the meetings of God's holy people. (1 Corinthians 14:33)*

Kay and I have found that during these tunnel times we find peace only in the Word of God, not through our neighbors or friends or family. All of these people are important, but ultimately it breaks down to God's plan for my life and often for our lives together. Sure, like you, we become overwhelmed, our hearts race, and our minds become somewhat frantic. But:

> *Then you will experience God's **peace**, which exceeds anything we can understand. His*

*peace will guard your hearts and minds as you
live in Christ Jesus. (Philippians 4:7)*

Yes, live in Christ and He will give you the peace that passes all understanding! I want to end this segment with a message from the Apostle Paul. When you follow his time on earth, Paul spent more time in the tunnel than out.

He was continually persecuted for his allegiance to Jesus Christ. As you are working through your tunnel, listen to this final greeting in his letter to the Thessalonians.

*"Now may the Lord of **peace** himself give you
his **peace** at all times and in every situation.
The Lord be with you all." (2 Thessalonians
3:16)*

And I say may the Lord be with you all as well.

## Tearing Down Our Confidence

So far we have had some pretty direct talk about God's control in your life, and we've had a few laughs as well. But I know some who are reading this book are in such a dark tunnel that my words and my humor do not give you relief. You might say, "Bob if you only had my challenge, you would not be able to write what you have written." Please hear me when I say empathetically and emphatically, "I do understand." So many reading these words at this very moment are so tired of the fight, the day in and day out treadmill of just surviving—perhaps in what you might think is a hopeless battle, a doomed relationship with your mate or friend, or a battle with your kids.

Let me take a moment and share one of our darkest tunnels, a tunnel that lasted over twenty years. My wife and I went through this one together, and it was during this time most everything I have written became real to us.

I wish to share this story in hopes that it will help others as they are either personally in this tunnel or have a loved one in the tunnel.

## Drugs and Alcohol

I had been living my renewed life in the Lord for about 13 years. I've told you about some of the crazy challenges Kay and I faced, but we weathered each challenge and matured in our faith. However, our biggest and longest test (our darkest tunnel) came when our 18-year-old son began using drugs and alcohol. You know there is something different about you and your wife having personal challenges compared to when one of your children has a challenge. I can't really explain it, but those of you who have children know what I am talking about. At first we were in denial; we tried to convince one another that this would go away, that this was just that unique time of life for him.

Surely God would not allow this to happen to us. We were living the "this can't be happening to me syndrome" I defined earlier. As our son's disease progressed, we began the conversation with God: "Why would you let this happen to us? Lord, we raised our son in a Christian environment; he was home schooled and then we enrolled him in a private Christian school, so Lord give us a break." Then we got on the roller coaster of emotions—being mad at our son and telling him to either quit or not come around this home any longer. Since I was educated in the school of **Get Over It Now** (like many fathers), my response was "get over it!" Then we went through the **It's Your Choice** school with him. You know, where you tell him he is making bad choices and he knows better. Something like "We brought you up better than your current behavior." Then we sent him to **Guilt School**—"Don't you see how your actions are creating challenges for your sisters?" When that didn't work, we tried the **Health School**; "Do you have any idea what you are doing to your body when you use drugs and alcohol?"

Then we joined the **Spiritual School**. Surely this would work. "Son, you are a Christian. The Word of God is clear. You are not to exhibit this behavior; you are not living the fruit of the Spirit." Or "Do you not know that your body is a holy temple for God? What are you doing to His temple?" As a last resort, we left him at the **Hardball School**. "Get out of this house with your drugs and alcohol, and do not come back until you get a handle on it." Sadly, at this point I physically threw my son out of the house. We went to God in prayer, saying things like "Lord, please heal my son." "God you know our hearts, and this is not what you want." My wife cried so many times that she actually ran out of tears.

We were limp and totally defeated. All the conversation in the family was about our son and the negative impact he was having on the family. But it was at this hour that my wife and I looked at each other and simply said, "God has control. There is nothing we can do. We will either bury him or see him healed, but either way it is in God's hands."

Even though we released him, the battle hadn't even begun. We would get call after call from our son each evening. He spent hours telling us how he was going to kill himself. He would be totally blown away with alcohol.

My wife received a phone call from a drug dealer who simply said, "I know where you live, and I will find you." We assumed our son owed the dealer money, and he was threatening us to get our son to pay. The pain can never be explained. We would work hard to have a normal life, but there was never an hour when one of us was not thinking about our son. My wife took it very hard; I do believe it is harder on the mother than the father. The mother keeps flashing back to the baby she carried in her body, the birth, and the little child she once enjoyed. Over the next several years, we put our son in five rehabs with no positive results.

Sometime in late 2008 or early 2009, I was asked to speak on leadership at a university in Tulsa. Rob's battle had gone on for twenty years, and although we had moved to Houston, he still lived in Tulsa.

While I was speaking, my wife felt led to find our son, and after making many calls, she located him. We asked him to join us for dinner, and he came, but he was totally out of it—high and incoherent. One of his closest friends came with him, someone who was working to help our son through this disease.

The next day we went over to Rob's apartment. It brought me to tears; here was our son, lying on the floor in his living room, no furniture, a table fan on the floor, and a TV. He was having convulsions, and he was literally out of his mind with alcohol. My wife and I looked at each other, and without any conversation simply picked him up and said, "Son, you are going with us back to Houston." I leaned over and told my son, "Rob, it is time. You have to go with us." With tears in his eyes he said, "Dad, I need help." Kay and I are confident that if God had not brought us to his apartment that day, our son would have died.

We put all of his belongings in a couple of pillowcases. It broke my heart to think that my only son's total life belongings could be put in pillow cases. And away we went to Houston.

Not knowing what to do, my wife got on the phone calling a rehab we had heard about on television. It was a no-nonsense facility (the type where they shave your head and scream at you 24 hours a day. Most of those in this rehab are former inmates who have been told you either go to this rehab or back to prison). They said they would take him, but they would not take him until he was totally detoxed.

For the next three days, we worked on detoxing our son. Those of you who have been through it, you know the agony. Kay and I prayed daily for wisdom from God, and we kept reminding each other that "God is in control!"

I knew that if we were to have any chance in the process, I had to totally focus on our son, and I begin researching the "why" behind his problem. Kay and I came to the conclusion that that we had to sell our business and focus on this challenge.

We had an extremely lucrative business, and my business partner almost fell out of his chair when I shared that I had to leave and put my total focus on our son. We believe this decision was God-inspired as we searched for His wisdom in this tunnel.

We more or less warehoused our son while I went to work looking for answers to the disease of alcohol. I would spend late hours on the Internet, and I would call the heads of major rehab facilities and drill them for answers. I contacted authorities in the field and asked them what could be done.

I visited with many PhD's in psychology at a number of rehab facilities as they shared their personal opinions. During my research, I discovered that there are two schools of methodology related to alcohol problems—one being what is known as "talk or behavioral therapy." This is where the therapist asks questions about your past and how perhaps certain "triggers" cause you to turn to alcohol.

Their approach is from the psychological side of reasoning. The other theory was one unfamiliar to me. The treatment works from the position of bringing the body back into harmony, believing that most of the challenge stems from nutrition, a more holistic approach.

My research brought me to a facility in Minnesota where I sat down and spent a couple of hours with the founder who had lost her son to alcohol. After that visit and my continued research into alcoholism as a "disease" rather than a "behavioral issue," I chose to move forward in the direction of restoring the body. The facility in Minnesota was an outpatient community, and I knew that my son was not capable of functioning as an outpatient. So we found an inpatient facility that offered what I believed to be the best resource, and we moved our son to that facility.

Now let me stop for a moment and take you to what was happening spiritually during this time. Kay and I were driven to read the Word and to search for deeper truth. During this trip, we had to get a **GRIP.** We had to move from the **emotional** to the **spiritual** world. So often when negative things appear in our lives and we find ourselves in the tunnel of major challenges, all of our reactions are **emotional**. We listen to the words of those around us instead of the living Word of God. We had to acknowledge that **God was in control**! We **rejoiced** during the challenge in order to release stress and lift up praise to a God in control.

Oh, how we **initiated our faith**. As Kay says, we had to believe something was so when it was not so, so it could be so. My lovely wife says "faith and fear cannot reside in the same house." Faith removes fear. And finally, our **prayers** were not for healing but for wisdom. "Dear God, show us your deeper purpose for this trial in our life and our son's life. Show us the wisdom needed to respond to our son and to those who are working with him."

**GRIP** immediately sets things in motion that will make the tunnel time a little easier.

Now I am not saying all fear fades away. No, just as our Lord had great fear prior to his crucifixion (such that he sweat blood in the garden), you too will find yourself late at night or in the early morning hours sweating and finding fear approaching your mental doorway. But just as Christ took action when He spoke, "Not my will but your will be done," we can repeat the same words in our tunnel. "My Lord, not my will but Your will be done." Folks I don't even want to pretend this is easy. For in these times we are weak and mentally depleted of the ability to reason.

I am not from the "power of positive thinking school." But I am a positive thinker based upon what the Word of God teaches our attitude must be to sustain us during times of trial. He observes our attitudes.

> But my servant Caleb has a different **attitude** than the others have. He has remained loyal to me, so I will bring him into the land he explored. His descendants will possess their full share of that land. (Numbers 14:24)

Viktor Frankl was an Austrian neurologist and psychiatrist who was also a Holocaust survivor. He lived through and witnessed nearly every inconceivable atrocity humans can sustain, and yet he survived. His mother, father, and wife were all killed in the camps. He witnessed starvation, torture, and the murder of his friends. My friends, this is a tunnel few of us can even fathom. He writes:

> "Everything can be taken from a man but one thing: the last of the human freedoms— to choose one's attitude in any given set of circumstances, to choose one's own way." (*Man's Search for Meaning*)

> *Instead, let the Spirit renew your thoughts and* **attitudes**. *(Ephesians 4:23)*

Moving forward through our decades-long tunnel, I wish I could say that our son came out of rehab cured and all ended well. About one year after he left rehab, he relapsed.

What we thought was a dark tunnel was like light gray compared to where we were headed. He became very tired all the time, and so we took him to a doctor who told us he needed to increase his testosterone level. So they gave him injectable steroids. His behavior became strange as he experienced panic attacks and sleepless nights. He would be up one day and down the next. His behavior became very unpredictable.

So we took him to another doctor who said his problem was an overload of testosterone, and he needed to come down off that medication. This doctor's answer was that he was bi-polar. So the new regime was to be three major drugs—one to take him up, one to take him down, and one to help with sleep. Our son was living with us so we could stay on top of his challenge. All of a sudden, he actually went crazy, coming downstairs in a rage and then seeing things. He would say, "Do you see them? Be careful; they are out there." He would be in total fear. Our tunnel then took us to a psychiatric hospital where they simply tried to change his prescriptions. (I would like to say to doctors: **Rule Number One**— Find out if the patient is a drug or alcohol abuser before handing out these simple little pills.)

The tunnel continued to get darker and darker and darker. He began looking for my guns, making videos saying goodbye, on, and on, and on.

Not only were we in the tunnel, but the train had stopped with absolutely no end in sight and no light. During this time we became stronger and stronger. We went to war with our enemy; we would call out his name and demand he leave our home and our son. While we were in the tunnel, God began to show us something I call **spiritual strength**. I remembered a passage I read when I first became a Christ-follower:

> *"Put on all of God's armor so that you will be able to stand firm against all strategies of the devil. For we are not fighting against flesh-and-blood enemies, but against evil rulers and authorities of the unseen world, against mighty powers in this dark world, and against evil*

*spirits in the heavenly places." (Ephesians 6:11-12)*

While we were in the tunnel, God showed us the real enemy, and we began to stand between our son and the enemy. We claimed victory (even though we saw no sign of it). We claimed deliverance (even though it was not manifested). We simply began to line up with what we teach:

- **God** is in control!
- We will **rejoice** in times of trouble!
- We will **initiate our faith** muscle (believing something is so when it is not so, so it can be so)!
- We will **pray** for wisdom—over and over and over again!

And now we will fight the spiritual war we are facing. We knew that Christ defeated Satan with "His blood, the cross, and the Word." So we would often pray *"Father, in the name of Jesus, we cover our son with Your precious blood. We bring forward Your cross to rebuke the negative spirits attacking our son, and we speak the Word, as Jesus said when He was tempted by Satan himself, 'Get behind Me Satan.' "* And we would quote Scripture. *"Greater is He who is in My son than he who is attacking My son."*

Folks, I am not saying this is your formula for your tunnel, but I do know that God is waiting to give you His formula if you seek His wisdom. God's plan is not the same for all of us, for each of us will be given our own personal instruction book for each tunnel, instructions that will meet our needs and lead to His adoration. Kay and I have found that what God shows us is not necessarily what He will show you at your time of need, but we are confident He will meet you at your point of need and give you the peace of mind needed to move through your personal tunnel.

> *I am leaving you with a gift—peace of mind and heart. And the peace I give is a gift the world cannot give. So don't be **troubled or afraid.*** (*John 14:27*)

This chapter in our son's story concluded with his decision to get off all the medicines that had been prescribed for him, and after several weeks his body began bringing itself back into balance.

As he began to get better, he returned to the psychologist who diagnosed him as bi-polar. The doctor reversed his findings and wrote a letter saying our son was not bi-polar (and get this) and that all of his problems were **doctor induced**! In essence, the prescriptions given to our son had only created more problems.

He is now drug and alcohol free, working and doing very well as a personal trainer. He has found a lovely young lady who loves the Lord, and he is daily thanking our God for His grace in his life. He has learned how to "manage" his disease just as a diabetic would manage their disease.

More important, as we have come out on the other end of this tunnel, we see how God is using our experience so Rob and Kay and I can assist the many who are headed for this particular tunnel. Without Christ, I fear what would have happened to us as a family, but the glory is to God. He is faithful and just to those who love Him. (Amen brother Bob! Get out the Kentucky Fried Chicken™ buckets, and let's take a large offering.)

# 4

ENDURE
+ENCOURAGE
+EMPOWER
+EQUIP

*"And endurance develops strength of character, and character strengthens our **confident hope** of salvation." (Romans 5:4)*

I just received a call from a publisher who wanted to know what my new book is about, how many chapters it has, and why people would be interested in reading the book. He asked about areas of price point, how many chapters would be necessary, and the all-important word count (how many total words). I often laugh under my breath when talking to these folks, thinking about what they would say about the Bible. Can you imagine a publisher calling the Apostle Paul, "Now Mr. Paul, we have to be sure the book appeals to a certain demographic. It can't be over so many words and must be sent to us in a Word document as we do not accept scrolls."

I am not as concerned about the word count as I am that the words I write "count." It is my prayer and my wife's that this book will be a simple read but one that can give you the light you are looking for in your tunnel—a place of refuge where you can seek input from a couple who have been in multiple tunnels and found **peace of mind** while going through them.

I know it will be hard for many of you to believe, but I did not do well in certain subjects in high school or college. Let's just say, if it were not for me, many of you would not have been in the upper 3%. Because of me, your status was elevated. The sciences were never good to me; some professor would sit down with me and try to improve my understanding of something like Newton's

Law of Universal Gravitation. I did not need a formula to understand gravity; I fell off a ladder when I was 9 years old and understood the subject quite well.

I will begin this chapter with a formula that I am sure does not make any sense whatsoever when you first look at it.

So let's break it down (cue the music—break it down, break it down). We have already driven by that nasty word "**endurance**" in this book.

Just saying the word makes you want to curl up in a ball and pull the covers over your head. **ENDURE**—we must hang on in our pain!

Often people will ask me why they must go through tunnels. It is fascinating to hear the definitive and confident answers many pastors or believers give. It is as if they understand the purposes of God. Here is my answer: **I don't know**!

I can hardly wait to get to heaven, for I am sure God will put me in a viewing room, turn down the lights, and begin running a film of my life, showing me all the scenarios that might have been.

Somewhat scary, huh? I do not have all the answers for you, but here is what Kay and I have learned and what we believe our tunnels have taught us.

Without endurance you cannot become stronger in your faith.

*"We can rejoice, too, when we run into problems and trials, for we know that they help us develop **endurance**." (Romans 5:3)*

Our tunnel experiences, just like yours, were major problems and trials, and each time we received a first-hand lesson on endurance. You see, a diamond is nothing more than a large chunk of coal until it is put under pressure. I am more than confident that our tunnels are engineered by God to check our endurance, to humble us, and to test our character to determine if we are trusting God.

*And **endurance** develops strength of character, and character strengthens our confident hope of salvation. (Romans 5:4)*

Character: Moral or ethical strength. Isn't it true that each time we go through a tunnel and come out on the other side, we are stronger? My wife and I have been tested multiple times in multiple tunnels, and I can assure you we have grown through each experience. And as this scripture says, each time the experience brought us back to the "confident hope of salvation." For without Christ all is hopeless and futile.

Endurance also allows us to receive more power through Christ.

*"We also pray that you will be strengthened with all his glorious power so you will have all the **endurance** and patience you need. May you be filled with joy." (Colossians 1:11)*

We can honestly attest to the fact that each tunnel has given us more character, strength, and patience, and each time we have found praise and joy. Try to explain that to an Aggie. Since I am a former Aggie, I have earned the right to pick on Aggies. I am not saying Aggies are slow learners, but many years ago I went over to visit my friend Larry Don. He was a linebacker on our football team. When I entered his house, I noticed his right ear was burned to a crisp. I said "Larry, what happened, my friend?" "Bob, I was ironing my shirt and the phone rang!" I said, "OK, I understand, but why is your other ear also burned to a crisp?" "Well, Bob, that silly fool called back."

Endurance, do I totally understand it? Nope! Do I accept it? Yup! For I have been told that it comes from Christ.

> *"May the Lord lead your hearts into a full understanding and expression of the love of God and the patient **endurance** that comes from Christ." (2 Thessalonians 3:5)*

**Our tunnel experience increases our endurance, but why the need for endurance? God does strange things here on the earth since He doesn't communicate like the speaker at a** Sonic drive-in. (If you do not have a Sonic in your hometown, I doubt if you are living in America. If you do and have not tried the foot-long Coney, the chances you will go to heaven are slim to none.) Since God has no megaphone, He uses people. What Kay and I have learned in life is that success is an identity process, meaning that many of the tunnels we endure allow us the ability to identify with others who are in that same tunnel or headed for that tunnel. Why? Thought you would never ask. It brings us to the second "E."

## Encourage

Kay was 15 and I was 17 when we met, and now **we have been married for over 47 years.** Since we have been married that many years, it would be difficult for us to provide meaningful encouragement to someone who is experiencing a divorce. That isn't something we have endured, so our attempts to encourage might not be very significant.

Yes, we could share our faith. Yes, we could offer guidance on what the Word of God says. But reassurance would be more meaningful if it came from someone who has gone through the experience and come out victorious on the other side. Kay and I know the pain of having a child on drugs and alcohol; we understand the pain of complete financial collapse; we understand the waiting to determine the results of a serious medical test; therefore, we can **encourage** someone entering one of those tunnels with the **confident hope** that they will survive.

My heart hurts for those whose children have died in the battle with drugs or alcohol because I've been in that battle. Today during my wife's Bible study, she learned of a young mother who took her newborn baby to a hospital, dropped it off, and overdosed just a few hours later. We know that tunnel.

A very close friend of ours from Minnesota contacted us one evening and shared that her son did not make it through the tunnel of drugs. He had passed away. We immediately got on a plane and went to her side. I shall never forget when her front door opened how she fell into my arms sobbing.

The pain was overwhelming. The hurt—it was more than I had experienced, but because we have been in the tunnel of drugs and alcohol, we could encourage. During the next few hours we talked about her son's many attributes and how he fought but lost. As we prayed with her on our departure, our prayer was that God would comfort her and her family and give her the endurance to move forward, to perhaps give her a peace and understanding on how this messed up puzzle would somehow fit together.

I am excited to say that God has used this mother in a mighty way, far beyond what Kay and I can offer. Her son's death planted a spirit in her heart to comfort and consult with as many parents as possible and to specifically be able to minister to the parents who have physically lost their child to the war with drugs and alcohol.

Yes, for sure she misses her son more than you can imagine. She will remember the day she lost him until she is reunited with him in heaven. But she has allowed God to take control of the situation and show her how she can minister to the thousands of mothers and fathers, brothers and sisters, aunts and uncles, and grandchildren as a result of her tragedy. When I reflect on the words we have used thus far: character, strength, patience, endurance, and faith— if we could put an equal sign after all these words, it would read "Gloria Englund." Praise God for his **grace** and **peace** on her life as she moves forward with her mission.

Gloria has come through her tunnel stronger and with passion and focus to help people related to drugs and alcohol. If you are faced with losing a loved one to drugs, I recommend you contact Gloria at www.recoveringu.com. Gloria is a person who shares great encouragement!

Kay and I have a wonderful friend, Gary Richardson, a very successful trial attorney in Tulsa, Oklahoma. He has been credited with winning the largest jury verdict for slander ever awarded in United States history— $58,000,000.

More important than his success is his heart toward God. Gary understands more than most the significance of God's sovereignty. We love sitting down with Gary, for we are like three computers plugged together as we talk about challenges and how God is in total control. One of his books is entitled *Fear is not our Friend*. I suggest everyone order this book and read it a couple of times. Gary makes a statement that seems worthy of repeating as we move forward: **adversity has a beautiful way of introducing us to ourselves.**

What a great statement! I must say, I hate it when someone comes up with a great maxim I didn't think of first; however, when you are in your next tunnel, repeat that statement three times, and I am confident you will view your tunnel experience much differently.

As we segue to our next thought, I need to set it up with a little story. Before my friend Zig Ziglar's passing, I received a phone call from his personal assistant.

Zig was finishing his new book, and they wanted to know if I would consider doing a video interview with his son, Tom, talking about Zig and his new book, *Born to Win*. It was a real honor as I joined the ranks of several good men and women around the world paying tribute to my mentor, Zig Ziglar. In my interview with Tom, I made the following comments: "Mr. Zig is much like the Apostle Paul, in that Paul spent his entire life **encouraging, empowering** and **equipping** people. Zig has done the same over his many years, and I am proud to say I am one of his students who will continue the process of building people up, and helping them to see their importance in the eyes of God." We must never stop encouraging others!

### Heart in Your Throat

Have you ever experienced a "heart in your throat" moment? You know, when what is happening to you is so traumatic you feel your heart jump straight up to your throat.

As I shared earlier, after my flight adventure with my son, I was determined to get my instrument rating. Now for those of you who are not familiar with airplanes and how a person receives an instrument rating, let me share some brief details. The takeoff is normal. You taxi out on the runway, get cleared for takeoff by the tower, and give the plane full throttle. In a training airplane, this means you are moving just beyond the speed of the resident turtle walking down the runway beside you. You pull back on the yoke (that being the wheel) and up you go. Almost immediately, the instructor who is sitting next to you in the right seat has you put on a hood that covers all of your outside view. The only thing you can see is the instrument panel in front of you.

During this time, he is continually giving you instructions: left bank, right bank, power on stall, power off stall, over and over and over.

A good instructor, like the one I had, continues to encourage you through each step. Then comes the day you have heard other pilots speak of. He reaches over and flips your hood down so all you can see is your knees—no instruments whatsoever. He takes the controls and begins to put the plane through multiple maneuvers, banking the plane left and right, gaining altitude, and lowering the nose to decrease altitude. All of the maneuvers are very gentle, and you feel you have a pretty good idea of the position of the airplane. Then he says, "Bob, on the count of three I am going to take my hands off the yoke and my feet off the rudder and hand it back to you." He instructs you to calmly raise your hood so you can only see the instruments without looking outside to bring the plane back to a level flight. I am thinking, what does he mean back on level flight? It feels level to me! He wants you to experience what is known as "vertigo."

This is where the brain has become disoriented, making you totally unaware of the flight path and attitude of the airplane. "OK Bob, 1-2-3. You are now in control. It's all yours."

I looked at my instrument panel—a quick look at my attitude indicator which would tell me the angle of plane, whether I am gaining or losing altitude, if I am in a bank, and if so, to what degree. Immediately, my heart jumped to my throat, my adrenaline was rushing, and I broke out in a cold sweat as I looked at my artificial horizon to see what was happening. This sadistic flight instructor had set the plane in a power-on stall at a 30° bank, and immediately when I took over the controls the plane began to drop like a rock! I could hear a chuckle as he watched me hold back my breakfast and keep my jeans from going over my head as I quickly brought the airplane back to level flight. I had only seconds to determine what to do as fear swept over my body and I was forced to respond to a very unnatural challenge.

This maneuver is done multiple times along with other high blood pressure exercises like pulling your throttle back while you are instructed to locate the closest airport for an emergency landing at 10pm. He once asked me, "Bob, what is the proper procedure should you lose power at night?" (My first response was to be sure and wear dark slacks so no one could see the stain if I survived.)

He continued, "It is a very simple procedure. Set the airplane up in a 500 feet per minute descent, relax, and then about 200 feet above the ground turn on your landing lights. If you do not like what you see, turn them off." Oh, what encouragement!

Many of you are having a "heart in your throat" experience at this very moment as you are entering your tunnel. Your nervous system is on overdrive, your breath has been sucked out of your lungs, and you sense fear like you have never experienced before.

Your mind is racing through your list of negatives: what if, what shall I do, how will I survive, where do I go, who can offer help? It is like going through a railway tunnel at night. The walls of the tunnel may have lights every ten feet, but as the train moves through the tunnel, all you can see is flash after flash almost like a laser beam of high speed light. This is the speed you feel your brain is moving as millions of fearful thoughts move through your mind.

You feel totally out of control, and yet you have this inner thought that you must remain calm and recover quickly for the sake of those who rely on you, perhaps your kids, mate, or family member.

My dear friend, if I could be close to you at this moment, I would offer these words: I know it is tragic for the moment. I do understand the fear and the hopelessness, the doubt and lack of confidence as to whether you will survive this tunnel, the questions—how can I go on, how can I remain strong? When you are tired and weak is when God becomes strong and offers encouragement.

> *With this news, strengthen those who have tired hands, and **encourage** those who have weak knees.  (Isaiah 35:3)*

Oh, how many times can we say our knees become weak as we enter the tunnel or as we go through the tunnel, and how much more do we need to encourage others and be encouraged ourselves?

> *"When we get together, I want to **encourage** you in your faith, but I also want to be **encouraged** by yours." (Romans 1:12)*

I see it only fitting to close with the words of Apostle Paul:

> *"Dear [Bob and Kay—He actually said brothers and sisters, but insert your name], I close my letter with these last words: Be joyful. Grow to maturity. **Encourage** each other. Live in harmony and peace. Then the God of love and peace will be with you." 2 Corinthians 13:11*

Wonderfully said, Mr. Paul, wonderfully said!

### Empower

I am more than confident that if we keep our eyes on Christ, get a **GRIP**, and forge forward, we will soon see that our tunnel experience has a higher purpose. Once we have gained **endurance**, we can **encourage** others as they move through their personal tunnel. Because of our tunnel (even though it was and is painful), our ultimate goal has become to **empower** others by sharing our personal journey. It is now time to see how our formula allows us the ability to **empower** others.

Let me tell you a story that illustrates this principle. There once was a young man who returned from military service shortly after the Vietnam War. He didn't know what to do with his life, so he decided that college might help him to investigate his options for the future. Since he had been away from studies for quite some time, he decided to ease into academics with some courses that would provide an easy reentry: Psychology 1111, American History 1111, Speech 1111, and a physical education class. In no time, he discovered that the classes were boring, and he deemed the subject matter relatively useless.

However, he did get somewhat excited about his speech class with a professor who was easygoing and whose emphasis on the importance of proficient speech made a tremendous amount of sense. There were 300 students in the class, and they took attendance by simply checking the empty seats. But out of all these students, for some incredible reason the professor seemed drawn to this young veteran, and in a short period of time, they became friends. One day they met during lunch in an unlikely place—the engineering and mathematics building on campus. As they walked the hallways from the top floor to the bottom, the professor observed that this was the building housing the highest IQ's on campus. Many of the students who studied here would leave the university to become some of America's greatest scientists, mathematicians, and engineers. However, for the most part, he argued, they would never have the ability to succeed financially due to their inability to clearly express their convictions and ideas.

If the young man were motivated to stay in class and apply the principles he would learn, the professor promised him that his success would parallel the university's brightest and best, and that perfecting his communication skills could bring financial rewards that would surpass anything he could dream of.

The semester ended with the young man sticking it out and doing quite well in the class. A few weeks later, the professor went to Dallas, Texas, for a seminar where someone broke into his hotel room, tied him up, and murdered him. What a tragic story with a potentially tragic ending, except that the ultimate tunnel experience the professor endured not only influenced the young man but empowered him to move forward becoming a professional speaker, writer, and leadership coach. The professor was Dr. Dale Stockton from Oklahoma State University. And that young man was me.

You see my friends, God uses multiple ways to empower people, to influence people, and to raise people up. As tragic as the death of Dr. Stockton was, God used it to empower Bob Goshen. And because of our tunnel (even though it was and is painful) our ultimate goal has become to empower others by sharing our personal journey.

*"I pray that from his glorious, unlimited resources he will **empower** you with inner strength through his Spirit." (Ephesians 3:16)*

I can't help but think again of Gloria, the mother who lost her son to drugs. God has used her to empower and influence others. Read the multiple Bible stories from Noah, to Moses, Jesus, Paul, John the Baptist, and so many others; they were used by God to empower thousands in the past and influence us today as we face our tunnels.

Yes, I realize what you are going through is not pleasant. I know that many of you reading this book are reading it through tears, that your life has been tragic up to this point. Some of you may see no way out of your tunnel, maybe you feel anguished and desolate, perhaps even despairing of life. You may be at a major crossroads, receiving negative health news, discovering the unfaithfulness of a mate, going through the last stages of divorce, financial failure, or trapped in the world of alcohol and drugs.

**Listen to me**; please understand that there is nothing happening to you that has not happened to others, and millions have come out on the other side as victors rather than victims. Whether you are a child of God or still searching for truth, your tunnel does not surprise the Lord. He empowers you with a way of escape. The temptations (problems) you are experiencing have been well thought out:

> *"The temptations* [problems] *in your life are no different from what others experience* [pretty well kills the ol' poor me]. *And God is faithful. He will not allow the temptation* [problem] *to be more than you can stand. When you are tempted, he will show you a way out so that you can endure." (1 Corinthians 10:13)*

## Equip

It was spring football practice at Oklahoma State University. Spring in Oklahoma is normally pretty humid and hot. We would suit up in the locker room, and while waiting for the coaches to come out, we sat outside on the benches with our helmets off— absorbing the last breeze we would feel for the next three hours. I hated the baseball players; they would walk by us in their shorts and t-shirts, drinking their cold Coca-Cola's (I've disliked baseball ever since). Our coaches would come out and begin to shout, **"Let's hit it boys! Time to sweat!"** And oh how we did. When I played football, you were considered a baby if you asked for water (real men don't ask for water—they would rather call an ambulance). No matter how much we hurt, we never complained. The motto was: "If it ain't broken (as in bones), move on." Another reason we did not complain was that our trainer had only one leg, and we were told he cut it off himself during the war. (To this day, I don't know if that story was true, but for sure you never complained about blisters or fractures.)

One spring day, my linebacker coach had all the linebackers gather at the end zone to go through what is known as the goal-line defense. This is how you line up when the football is within three yards of your goal line. As linebackers, we would get on the line of scrimmage with the defensive tackles. My assignment was to bury my helmet in the dirt (mud during the rainy season) and get as low as possible as another linebacker would climb my back (football cleats feel wonderful in the small of your back) and go over me to protect against any run up the middle. Our coach would have us repeat this drill over and over and over again. At one time I became so frustrated as he kept screaming **"Lower, Goshen. You have to get lower!"** I was thinking to myself, coach the only thing lower than me on this football field would be a gopher on the 20 yard line.

I finally lost my cool, jumped up, threw a hefty right hook at the coach, and yelled, **"You get down here and do it!"** Bad move. Rule number one: don't talk back to coaches.

Fortunately, I missed; however, he grabbed my facemask. This is not good, for if one has your facemask, one can move you wherever one wishes as the head must follow the helmet. He jerked my face to his face and began to shout (I remember his breath to this day—terrible garlic breath).

"Goshen," he yelled as he snapped my head toward the bench. "Are you not happy about being out here, son? Take a good look; over there are 42 boys that would love to be out here in your place! I am only demanding and shouting at you because I believe in you and have to **equip** you for the Saturday game! If you do not like me correcting you, then you have my permission to go over there and sit on that bench and have a lovely, quiet afternoon."

I was thinking to myself, "This most likely means I will not get a Christmas card from my linebacker coach."

A life lesson: at times when we feel defeated, at times when we feel totally out of control, at times when we are in our deepest tunnel, at this time God is your linebacker coach saying, "I am working for you to gain perfection; I believe in you, and yes it is hard at the moment, but you must be equipped in order that you might equip others."

> *God uses it* [your tunnel] *to prepare and equip his people to do every good work. (2 Timothy 3:17)*

Again, I know this may be a terrible time for you; however, look beyond the tunnel and know that God, our sovereign God, is not shocked by what is happening to you at this very moment, and through this time He is preparing you for the Saturday game—the game that is yet to come where you will be equipped to equip others. Kay and I now see that all of our tunnel experiences have given us the ability to encourage, empower, and equip others.

During the painful times, we did not see this. When you lose everything financially, you are not too concerned about equipping others. But today I share our experiences from the platform to equip others with the knowledge that even though you might be losing everything, you can make it, and God has everything under His control.

## Financial Setbacks

Many reading this book are currently under great financial stress. The tunnel of finances seems long and dark.

In 1973, Syria and Egypt would attack the tiny nation of Israel. It was called the miracle war since Israel had 200,000 soldiers vs. 700,000 from Syria and Egypt. In 16 days, Israel would defeat Syria and Egypt—an amazing feat. Since the United States assisted Israel through logistics and intelligence, the Arab Nations would immediately strike back at the United States through an oil embargo.

Oil coming into the United States was embargoed, and the oil that was allowed in received a 200% tariff. It was devastating. Lines at the gas stations were two to three miles long; the Dow Jones stock market crashed to 500, interest on business loans soared to over 15%. Home loans were at 16%, companies were declaring bankruptcy, and great people were going broke. I was a young entrepreneur at the time, owner of three companies. In two years, I went from being on top to hitting the bottom. I had to let my entire employee force go (one of the hardest things I have ever done).

Business dried up overnight, but the loan payments continued. For the first time in my life I was facing the possibility of bankruptcy. I contacted my banker and asked instead of taking bankruptcy would he work with me and allow me to liquidate all of my assets, furniture, fixtures, and equipment and let me take on the balance of the loan as personal debt. He agreed.

One of the most humiliating days of my life was the day I had a moving truck come to my office and pick up everything from trashcans to computers. We had an auction company send out a notice, and we moved all of the contents of my office to the ballroom at a local hotel. As I stood there and watched people swarm over my belongings, it became apparent my dream of ownership was coming to an end. Knowing it was over, the only thing I could do was add a little humor. I turned to my banker and said, "I can think of two things that went wrong in this business opportunity." He asked, "What were they?" I said, "When I made the loan at your bank, I thought you knew something about business." He asked, "What is number two?" To which I replied, "You thought I knew something about business."

The hardest part was yet to come. In a few days, the bank contacted me and said they were calling the note on our home loan since I was unable to keep up with the payments. They were going to sell the house and apply any equity to the amount of money I owed them.

We also owned a couple of cars financed through Chrysler. Chrysler called and said I could either voluntarily return the cars, or they would come out and pick them up.

We were about to be stuck with no money, no home, and no transportation. We refused to tell our parents about our problem; we knew they had their own issues. Kay was such a trooper. She just worked to keep my spirits up, and she would say, "God knows where we are." It was less than a week before Christmas, and for the first time in our lives we had no money for gifts for our kids. An ice storm hit Tulsa that morning, and in the evening all the roads were a sheet of ice.

I had pushed the repossession of the cars back until the first of the year, and like a fool I got out on the road to make a run to the shopping center about a mile away. Then it happened. I was leaving the shopping center when another car was turning into the parking lot, and the driver lost control on the ice and hit my driver's side front fender, mangling it. I just went limp, and under my breath said, "Lord, what else can happen?"

All of sudden, the gentleman jumped out of his car, apologizing and pleading with me not to call the police. He asked how much I thought it would cost to repair the damage. I responded, "Around $500.00." He immediately took out his wallet, handed me $500.00, and drove off. The repair was only $200.00, so all of a sudden we were going to have a very merry Christmas. To shorten the story, we lost our home. Kay reminds me we did not lose it. We knew where it was, we just no longer had it— or cars, or credit, or furniture. Lying in bed one night, I had asked Kay, "Honey, do you like this bed?" "Oh yes," she said. To which I replied, "Well enjoy it; Sears will be here tomorrow to get it!" She thought I was kidding.

For those of you who are in that dark tunnel of financial despair, please believe me when I say we understand. It is not fun. My wife can attest to the nights I would actually experience dry heaves, watching in fear as our finances dropped to below zero. I experienced cold sweats, and my body felt lifeless. So we do understand your position.

The phone calls from the creditors would never stop. One time a credit card company called and wanted a payment of $200.00. I said I could not pay them since I also owed MasterCard. The voice on the other end of the phone said, "We **are** MasterCard." I then responded, "Great! If you will raise my credit limit, I will pay you the money I owe you." They didn't laugh either. Knowing your agony and pain, I say that "this too shall pass." You will recover, and I will assure you that the knowledge you are receiving regarding finance will be worth more than a PhD—a lesson that even the Wharton School of Business cannot teach. You will get through this tunnel; God does have a way for your escape. And yes, the day will come when, like me and Kay, if you endure, you will be encouraging, empowering and equipping others with your personal story. So get a **GRIP,** and you will soon be out of this tunnel of dark despair at which time I expect an email sharing your story. You may contact me at bob@bobgoshen.com.

# 5

FEAR

*"This is my command—be strong and courageous! Do not be afraid or discouraged. For the LORD your God is with you wherever you go." (Joshua 1:9)*

It was a beautiful spring morning in Oklahoma. I work from home, and I would get up with the kids each morning. Kay would feed them, and I would drive them to school. On this particular morning, I told Kay I wanted her to take the kids to school since I needed to pay some bills. Kay got up, fed the kids, and left, and then I proceeded to get out of bed, jump into the shower, and go to my office at the back of the house. Since no one was around, I just slipped on a t-shirt with my Fruit of the Looms®. Trust me, Michael Jordon looks much better in his unmentionables. Having lost a couple of upper teeth playing that wonderful sport of football, I was required to wear an artificial partial (I love football) that I could put in and take out. And on this morning, I decided to leave it out.

So there I sat, working at my desk, clad in underwear, sans partial plate, and the pièce de résistance—my new afro. As I began to work, I got this feeling out of nowhere— "something's not right." Honestly, the hair on the back of my head (there's more on the back than on top) began to rise. Then I heard the front doorbell ring, and I thought, "This is not a good time to answer the door." Strangely, the persistence at the front door kept increasing. I moved around from my desk to the den where we had a fireplace, and I picked up the fireplace poker and moved toward the front door. Just as I rounded the hallway, two young men entered my house and immediately, with large bug eyes, began to explain how they were only looking for a phone to call about their car being broken down. Looking back, I can only imagine their thoughts as they met me face to face—all 225 damp, undressed, toothless, and permed pounds of me—holding a fireplace poker and ready to strike. Funny now when you think about it. Since I grew up on the rough side of Tulsa, I began to explain to the young men in no uncertain terms that they should back out quickly as I was not buying their lie.

They backed through the door, turned, and started running down the driveway. I immediately called the police, and within an hour they had caught the young men. They were going around the neighborhood forcing their way through the front doors of housewives who were home alone and robbing them of their jewelry. I later found out they both were armed with 357 pistols.

Fear. It engulfed me that morning, especially when I began to reflect that normally Kay would have been at home instead of me. But as fearful as that moment was, it is nothing like the fear you might be experiencing at this moment as you are caught in financial battles, relationship challenges, abuse at the hand of a mate or friend, or the ultimate—being told you have an incurable disease. The difference is that my fear with the two intruders was what I call an "adrenalin fear." It happens quickly and fades quickly. The other type of fear is a "lingering fear." No matter what you try to do, it never leaves. You might have that loved one who is addicted to drugs and alcohol, and you find yourself waking up each night at 3:00am with fearful thoughts of what might be happening to him or her.

You may be the wife who is being physically abused, and you currently are sitting at home watching the clock, waiting for your mate to come home and once again begin your night of terror. Perhaps you are in that week of waiting for the results of a biopsy which will determine your future health or the health of a loved one. Maybe you are living under the cloud of job uncertainty. I sometimes call this lingering fear "tunnel fear." You are in that tunnel of pain, of regret, and of terror. Unlike adrenaline fear, this fear hangs in your mind and torments you 24 hours a day.

I once asked myself (great conversation when it is just me and me) why I couldn't escape such thoughts. No matter how hard I tried, they continued to linger—negative visions entering my mind through my thoughts. Then I read this verse:

> For we are not fighting against flesh-and-blood
> enemies, but against evil rulers and authorities
> of the unseen world, against mighty powers in
> this dark world, and against evil spirits in the
> heavenly places. (Ephesians 6:12)

Hang with me now; you don't need to be looking in your closet or under your bed, no need to get paranoid. But if you know who your enemy is and how he operates, then you can defeat him. Notice this scripture says **rulers, powers, spirits,** and **authorities**—all being plural, not singular. The chances of any of us meeting Satan one-on-

one is one gazillion to one, but these little thought-beings are continually working in our heads. Remember in our previous chapter where we were talking about encouragement, empowerment, and equipping? Well our enemy works to discourage, disillusion, and defeat us in any way possible. Fact number one: **Fear is not from God!**

> *For God has not given us a spirit of fear and timidity, but of power, love, and self-discipline. (2 Timothy 1:7)*

A mighty war is going on for our minds, the Spirit of God on one side and on the other the negative spirits as described in Ephesians 6:12. Our enemy wishes to paralyze you and me with his best offensive tool—fear.

Just as those boys entered my home, fear is entering your home (your mind) at this time of trial. I do not care how spiritual you might be; our enemy knows how to create that sweat-crawling, gut-wrenching, hair-raising fear. You can begin getting a **GRIP,** but your enemy will work to control your mind, changing your focus from the present to thoughts of a negative future. The strategy of these little mind-creatures is simple, it is **thought dropping**. Not just any thoughts, but defeating thoughts. These little spirits want you to think these thoughts are yours, when in fact they are their thoughts. If they can make you accept these thoughts, they will control your actions and your life.

Here are a few of the thoughts they drop when you are in your tunnel:

- You can't do it; there is no way you will make it through this challenge.
- You have always been a loser, so why are you shocked now?
- I told you he is not the man you married, and you deserve better.
- From the beginning, you knew she would never make a good wife.
- You deserve what is happening to you; you are a pitiful person.
- Why are you surprised at what is happening? Nothing good ever happens to you.
- You will go broke and lose everything because you were never good at supporting your wife and kids.

Do you get the idea? Here are a couple more:

- Your relationship isn't working because you are a pitiful soul.
- You will never be successful. You are a disaster!
- Everything you have tried in the past has failed, so why try again?

These little guys have been dropping thoughts into the lives of folks since they and their leader, Satan, were kicked out of heaven. Satan is the author of lies beginning in the Garden of Eden when he told Eve it was okay to eat the apple. You see they do not want you to read the Bible and get knowledge, for knowledge is their enemy. As a matter of fact they will say, "No need to open the Bible. There is no way you can understand what it says." Well let's see what the Word of God says about "I can vs. I can't." When you are going through your tunnel, do all you can to focus on these words, make them your primary thoughts, and rebuke the negative thoughts of your enemy.

> *"For I can do everything through Christ, who gives me strength." (Philippians 4:13)*

> *"No, despite all these things, overwhelming victory is ours through Christ, who loved us." (Romans 8:37)*

> *"If you need wisdom, ask our generous God, and he will give it to you. He will not rebuke you for asking." (James 1:5)*

My friends, these are promises. You do have a place to go to receive wisdom. Do not let those around you influence your thinking toward the negative, recognize the source of the negative thoughts coming into your mind, fall on your face and **ask for wisdom**. Find those you know who are wise and seek their input.

> *Walk with the wise and become wise. (Proverbs 13:20)*

Those little sprits of evil want us to worry because worry creates doubt and doubt creates fear and fear is the number one paralysis to our faith. But yet the Bible says:

> *Give **ALL** your worries and cares to God, for he cares about you. (1 Peter 5:7)*

How many times have we heard the expression "you are going to worry yourself to death" only to have nothing happen, or if it did happen it was never as bad as we projected? We immediately fall into the trap of fear, but feast your eyes on the following:

> "I will give you peace in the land, and you will be able to sleep with no cause for **fear**." (Leviticus 26:6)

> "I prayed to the LORD, and he answered me. He freed me from all my **fears**." (Psalm 34:4)

I remember when, during our financial trials, I had to face my banker and the attorneys who were seeking to destroy us from every direction. I found refuge in the following:

> "The Lord is for me, so I will have no **fear**. What can mere people do to me?" (Psalm 118:6)

> "But all who listen to me will live in peace, untroubled by **fear** of harm." (Proverbs 1:33)

> "You can go to bed without **fear**; you will lie down and sleep soundly." (Proverbs 3:24)

Isn't this cool? How many times have you gone to bed only to stare at the ceiling in worry about what might happen the next day? When I read Proverbs 3:24, I would recite it each night over and over until I went to sleep. Even today, if I do not recite positive scripture, those little evil spirits will go to work on me.

If you are still not relating to what the Word of God says about fear, then hopefully this verse can cement the deal:

> *"And I am convinced that nothing can ever separate us from God's love. Neither death nor life, neither angels nor demons* [those little evil thoughts in your head], *neither our **fears** for today nor our worries about tomorrow—not even the powers of hell can separate us from God's love." (Romans 8:38)*

Romans 8:38 is the final volley, the last **big bang** at the Fourth of July show, the mother of all lodes, the **big burrito**! In this verse God has given us the ultimate protection for **any** tunnel experience.

God's love is the ultimate factor in our battle with fear. He assures us that any troubles today or tomorrow, those stinking little demons, are all subject to His love for you and me, and **they will not** separate us from His love!

Okay, Bob. I get it. But man it is so hard for me to let go and just trust. I understand. Listen, as I am writing this book, Kay and I are facing another large tunnel. (In God's eyes it is nothing more than a blip.) Remember, He separated the Red Sea faster than we can snap our fingers. So I do know where you are at this very moment. And even though I am writing these words, it does not make it easier even for ol' Bob. What makes it even somewhat tougher for me is that I have to live up to what I am writing and sharing with you, and I will tell you first hand it is a demanding task. Remember, "We **wrestle** not against flesh and blood, but against little thoughts that paralyze us." (1 Bobby 1:7— a little paraphrase of Ephesians.) The key word is **wrestle**. We are continually in a **wrestling match** while we live in this world. So we each have a choice—bow down to our opponent or be equipped to wrestle.

I look at two definite options: living in sweaty fear and worrying or relaxing in the hands of God, **knowing** He is in control and all that is happening is for my good and the building of my **faith**. I'm like you. I do not like it, do not enjoy it, and do not need it at this time in my life, but as my wonderful son repeats often, "It is what it is!" So like you, I face that choice—bow down to fear or look up to an almighty God who is in total control of my life.

This morning on the patio, my lovely wife of more than 45 years read me a story. She **is** lovely. People often have assumed she is my daughter. But back to the story:

> *Once an Ethiopian named Zerah attacked Judah with an army of 1,000,000 men* [one million] *and 300 chariots. They advanced to the town of Mareshah,* [where did they get these names?] *Asa deployed his armies for battle in the valley north of Mareshah. Then Asa cried out to the Lord his God, "O LORD, no one but you can help the powerless against the mighty! Help us O LORD our God, for we trust in you alone. It is in your name that we have come against this vast horde. O LORD, you are our*

*God; do not let mere men prevail against you!"*
*(2 Chronicles 14:9-11)*

One million men would be a pretty scary sight, right? That would be a **big tunnel** challenge! Asa was the current king of Judah, and when we listen to his words we get a pretty good understanding of how he handled his tunnel problem.

> *"O LORD, no one but you can help the powerless against the mighty!"*

Asa quickly acknowledges God's supreme power and sovereignty, the **G** of **GRIP**. What do we do when we enter our personal tunnels? We cry out, but normally the words are "God, why is this happening to me? God, how can I get out of this mess?" Isn't it strange, when we are in our tunnels we use the terms "me" and "I." But Asa says **no one but you God** can handle this tunnel. Also, notice it says he didn't whisper, but he **cried** out to God—not a passing prayer but a promising statement of faith.

> *"Help us, O LORD, our God, for we trust in you alone."*

I don't know about you, but I often have a tendency of trusting more in my way of escape than in God's way.

Get the picture? "We **trust** in you **alone**." Not you and something else, but you only. I don't trust in the person who is creating this tunnel, I don't trust in the doctor's prognosis of death, I don't trust in my in-laws (or outlaws). No. It is **uno-to-uno**, me and you God, you **alone**. I think you are getting the picture. Our tunnels are the "vast armies" that rise up against us. That army can be multiple things, but in the eyes of God what is important is not the challenge we are facing but how we **respond** to the challenge. Do we acknowledge Him supreme and sovereign and trust Him, or do we fall to fear and defeat?

So what happened to Asa? Later in the passage we are told that Asa's challenge with the million men was overcome by the Lord. His tunnel was cleared by God. But the next statement is what you and I must stay focused upon during our tunnel time:

> *Then the Spirit of God came upon Azariah son of Oded,* [I can hear the roll call in their elementary school. Azariah are you here? Oded are you here?] *and he went out to meet King Asa as he was returning from the battle* [returning from his tunnel]. *"Listen to me, Asa!"* [Listen to me, Bob] *He shouted. "Listen, all you people of Judah and Benjamin!* [All you people who are in or entering your tunnel.] **The LORD will stay with you as long as you stay with him! Whenever you seek him, you will find him. But if you abandon him, he will abandon you."** (2 *Chronicles 15:1-4)*

Once again, the Word of God prevails in giving us the "peace that passes all understanding." So all of you little evil spirits out there that have been defeated by the resurrection of Christ, we enter our tunnel knowing this tunnel is covered by the blood of Jesus, this tunnel is located at the foot of the cross, and by the name of Jesus we declare our faith during this tunnel time knowing that God is in control. For we know that the blood, the cross, and the name of Jesus make evil spirits run in fear.

When Satan tempted Jesus, each time the Lord quoted the Word of God by saying "As it is written" or "thus says the Lord," and then He would quote Scripture.

When you equip yourself with the blood, the cross, the name, and the Word, our little demonic friends can't stick around. They have a real problem when you remind them about how they were defeated at the cross.

# 6

# WHEN BAD THINGS HAPPEN TO GOOD PEOPLE

Why **do** bad things happen to good people? Here's another answer I can be sure of: **I don't know!**

Now, like you, I have heard all the sermons and commentary seeking to answer this question. Sadly, those answers often come from "experts" who have never experienced a major tunnel. We look at all the dying babies around the world, we look at the events of 9/11, we look at the innocent mom and kids killed in a drunk driving accident, we see godly people in our churches struggling with cancer; and we say why?

There are times when I have to kill my earthly intellect and just trust in God. I know it may seem like a "cop out," but I always remember the scripture where God says *"Your ways are not My ways and your thoughts are not My thoughts."*

What I do know is what I read in the Bible about adversity, and I have read the multiple accounts of godly biblical characters that experienced trouble.

We hear so much preaching today on the goodness of God and that if you do "this thing or that thing" then you will be blessed beyond your wildest dreams. I do agree that all favor does come from God. He is in control, remember? But I also realize that every disciple had a tough road ending in terrible death. Even closer to home, I have had family and friends suffer illness and death at very early ages. I often flash back to 9/11 and my memory of those planes flying into the World Trade Center buildings. And I think about the tsunami that hit Japan and the earthquake that devastated Haiti. And what about the innocent children and teachers that were killed in Connecticut? I am amazed to hear all the reasons people give to justify that incident, how they focus the blame on guns or mental health. But for Christ-followers, the answer is much clearer: it is **sin**. We must acknowledge that evil has existed since the fall of man in the Garden of Eden, and it will continue to raise its ugly head until the return of our Savior. God did not make us robots, but please understand that none of the events in our personal lives or the tragedies that we see on the news ever surprises God. Even during the tragedy that occurs in our personal life or the major events on a global scale, we must remember that **God is in control**—the **G** in our **GRIP**. I do not understand it, I do not like it, but each time these events occur, I am pushed closer to God seeking comfort and grace as it says in Job 36:15:

> *But by means of their suffering, he rescues those who suffer. For he gets their attention through adversity.*

I have to agree with this inescapable assertion: "He gets their attention through adversity." In my lifetime on earth, I have learned much more through adversity than through prosperity. Many times I've asked God why He was doing this or that to me only to discover that "I" was the reason for the adversity.

## You Called the Meeting

*People ruin their lives by their own foolishness
and then are angry at the LORD. (Proverbs
19:3)*

I remember the days when our children were in their preteens. Like all young children, their youthful indiscretion sometimes gave me a reason to offer correction. We had a small paddle from "Six Flags over Texas" that was used for correction—very light swats—but enough to let them know they were being disciplined. It still puts a smile on my face when I think of the times my youngest daughter, Ashlee, would put on five or six pairs of panties believing I would not notice. Our procedure was consistent; should our kids need correction, we would send them to their room with the promise that "I will be there shortly!" Naturally, we would let them sit in their room for 15-20 minutes to consider what they had done and anticipate the punishment that was coming. It's the same tactic my father used, and now I know that he spent that time in the living room laughing about my bedroom suffering. When I disciplined the kids, I would always enter the room, sit down on the bed in order to be at their level and say, "Ashlee, I did not call this meeting. Your poor judgment has created this meeting and the punishment that will follow."

Naturally, I would hear all the excuses for why she did what she did as she tried to find a way of escape. (Looking back, it is still humorous to me but still not to her.) I would carry out the punishment and then hold her while I explained how it hurt me to have to punish her and that God wanted better for her. She would cry for a while, and then we would hug and move on with life.

I share this story to say I now see that many of my tunnels have been the direct result of my poor decisions. Because I violated principles, I would end up calling the meeting of correction on myself. A good example (one of many) comes from the early years of my marriage. I made unwise choices in the use of money, and so I put our family at risk. I would acquire multiple credit cards, use them to the max, and when it came time to pay I often lacked the funds. Therefore, I received calls day and night from credit card companies asking for payment. Now, as I look back, it is funny how angry I got as I made excuses and looked for a way of escape when ultimately I had "called the meeting." When my credit score went to just this side of "mud," I would naturally find a way to make it the credit bureau's mistake rather than accepting the fact that due to my bad choices, "I called the meeting."

The really sad thing about this was that I would often go to God in prayer asking Him to get me out of this situation. I was just like Ashlee trying to avoid the consequences of poor choices.

Kay and I have been married for 47 years, and we dated and were engaged over the preceding four years. We both entered marriage purely on feelings rather than faith or knowledge. We entered the marriage not having faith in Jesus Christ; and therefore, we had continual battles and what I call mini-wars within the home. I did not look for a mentor or try to develop better life skills, so why should it be a surprise that we found ourselves ready to divorce after seven years? If a marriage is based upon lust rather than love, one can expect jealousy, bitterness, and envy to characterize the relationship. Why are we shocked when it doesn't work? We "called the meeting." If I went out after work with my friends every night and stayed out late enjoying adult beverages, why would I believe I could come home to a house of harmony? "I called the meeting" that caused division in my home.

But even when I was a man without Christ, I would often cry out to God to heal my marriage and make my wife the lady I needed (notice how that prayer was all about me and mine). Again, I was violating principles, but I felt that God wasn't helping me out.

I can go on and on with stories of how I called multiple meetings in my life that resulted from bad choices, and naturally, instead of taking personal responsibility, it was always my wife's fault, the fault of a business partner or friend, or something else that caused the problem. Looking back, I can easily say I was the one calling the meetings and creating the problems.

I have known Christ for over four decades, and I have many friends who profess to know Christ. I am amazed when I see some of those friends routinely making decisions that seem to be in opposition to the clear will of God or acting in ways that contradict the Word of God. Yet those same friends cry out to God, "Why is this happening to me?" We make multiple choices each day, many of them poor choices that create negative results in our lives, and then we run to God asking Him to get us out of our mess. God's Word gives us principles for managing our finances and resources, taking care of our bodies, building and sustaining relationships, and creating successful marriages; yet we violate these principles and experience severe emotional or physical pain. Then off we go running to God asking, "Why is this happening to me?" My friends, we called the meeting!

I recently read the story of a gentleman on death row who, while in prison, accepted Christ as his personal Savior. As the execution drew near, he was interviewed on television, questioned about the faith he had professed for over 12 years, and asked how many men he had mentored while he was in prison. And then the reporter asked if he thought it was fair that he was still going to die for his crime. His response was simple: "I did a terrible thing several years ago by taking a person's life. Even though I am forgiven by my Father in Heaven, I must now pay the consequences for the sin I created several years ago." In essence, he was saying "I called the meeting!"

As we look back over all of the tunnels we have experienced thus far in our lives, how many of them resulted from our "calling the meeting" with bad decisions or poor choices? Speaking for myself, I have to say many. So let's be careful about running to God when we enter a tunnel of our own creation. And for sure, let's not blame God for our bad choices.

## Bad Choices

I recently read a magazine article about decision-making that said we make 612 per day, 4,900 per week, and 254,800 per year. Think about that—some must be good and some not so good. I've already written about one of my worst choices—the day I flew in bad weather without an instrument rating . . . and nearly killed myself and my son. That day was affected by many choices. Like many things in life, it began well but ended up in major stress. In reality I (not God) put myself in a major tunnel. Think about this for a moment. What if we had crashed and my son and I died? Some people would ask, "Why did God do this to Bob and his son? He was so young and had so many good things happening in his life; why would God take him?" Yet I was the one who violated a multitude of principles that caused a near fatality, so why should God take the blame? I wonder how many times we actually call the meeting by violating principles or making poor decisions that leave our family asking "Why would God do this?" Hopefully, I am making my point. I am sure when we all enter heaven (if we are allowed to see what caused all the major disasters that plagued our planet) we will find that individuals "called those meetings" or that those meetings were the result of the sin nature of man.

## Happily Ever After . . . Not!

Ladies, if you are a professing Christian and yet you allow a man into your life and into your bedroom without marriage, welcome to an "I called the meeting moment." I am not sure if this choice is made out of desperation or naivety, but believing that a true relationship can be established without commitment just makes no sense. Allowing a man to move in and play husband is an "I called this meeting" choice. How can God honor such a relationship? My wife has a good friend who has two children with two separate men . . . neither within the benefit of marriage. Now she is allowing a third man into her home and life, all while professing to be a child of God and working diligently in her local church. She continues to complain to Kay about not being satisfied or happy in life. What am I missing here? Ladies, you are too valuable to allow a male take advantage of you and seduce you into believing that all will be well if he can "just move in." Sounds great: split the bills and bingo - one happy family. Sadly, more often than not, these men take advantage in other ways, and the woman ends up being the provider. Ladies, please understand that you never need to lower your standards to have a partner in life; never get so desperate as to allow this to happen to you. If a man can have anything he wants without a commitment, trust me, he will move forward at full speed ahead.

Men, if you are the kind of man who professes to be a Christian and yet you move in with a woman outside of marriage and you live off of her, you are less than a man, and I would have to question your relationship with a living God. I know these are harsh words, but gentlemen, God's Word says we are to be the stronger person. If you cannot bring a lady into your life in a Christ-honoring way, loving her as Christ loved His church, and seeing her as a gift given to you by God, you need to test your belief system.

Again, I am talking to men who profess to know Christ and yet live as men of the world. Surely I am not the only person who realizes the disaster that can happen when this is allowed. Can I get an "Amen?"

# 7

# THE MARRIAGE TUNNEL

Zig Ziglar was my mentor for many years, and even though he has passed away, I can still hear the voice that boomed at me in his conference room: *"Bobby, if men would treat their wives like they did when they were courting them, there would be no divorces."*

I would like to begin this chapter by sharing the story of my own marriage. As I recount this story and remember where I have traveled during my years of marriage, perhaps anyone currently in a dark marital tunnel, experiencing negative challenges with their mate, will find the "confident hope" that you can overcome any situation you are currently experiencing. Plus, if you become bored reading this roller coaster of events, hopefully at least my grandchildren will enjoy knowing about their Papi and Nana.

I have had the blessing of being married for over 47 years to a marvelous woman. She was 15 and I was 17 years of age when we met at a high school football game. So our total time together has been over 50 years when you include dating and engagement.

It was a brisk fall day when I walked up behind this short little blonde and looked over her shoulder as she watched a "B" squad football game. I was truly focused on the game, just looking over her shoulder and not really noticing her, until she turned around and physically ran into me. Wow! The sun was setting behind us, and when she turned into the sun, her beautiful green eyes glistened, and all I could say was "Hello, green eyes." She was shocked when she turned around and physically ran into me, and she walked away without saying anything. It took me less than an hour to find out her name was Kay; she was a sophomore which meant that she was two years behind me in school. Within a couple of weeks, I worked up the nerve to ask her out on a date, and even though I was a senior in high school, I was quite nervous being around the opposite sex—actually somewhat shy.

Our first date was to a high school play. I don't remember the name of the play, but I still remember the dress she wore that evening—a beautiful red one in stark contrast to her magnificent blonde hair. Even though I was classified as a super jock—lettering in baseball, basketball, and football—I was totally intimidated by Kay that evening.

There we sat in the high school auditorium, focused on the stage. However, I spent more time focusing on this beautiful blonde woman in her pretty red dress. She looked 100% better than Julia Roberts, red dress and all in *Pretty Woman*. I eventually worked up enough nerve to hold her hand (hard to believe today that it was a big deal). Now people would laugh about hand-holding being an issue; but when we were dating, I think we were more respectful of ladies, and we moved more slowly.

After only a week, I asked her if she would "go steady" with me. That's a term long forgotten, but it meant that we wanted to make a commitment that we wouldn't date anyone else.

It was fun times in high school—Kay and I would look forward to seeing each other daily. We'd walk with each other down the halls as we went to class, find each other for lunch, and squeeze in a short time together after school before I went to baseball, basketball, or football practice. Shortly I would meet Kay's parents, and just as shortly they made it clear that I was not good enough for Kay. They also made it clear that we were not to date, which immediately threw a monkey wrench into my plans. Consequently, my creative juices began to flow, and within a few phone calls I found three of my friends who would pretend they were dating Kay. They would pick her up and then drive down to the local "Dairy Queen" where they would pass her off to me, and we would arrange a time to meet them so they could drive her home.

It's no wonder I ended up as a spy in the Navy. I was involved in clandestine operations at age 17.

This routine lasted two years until I made a major mistake (not as clever as I thought I was). It happened on Kay's prom night. By this time, I was attending Oklahoma State University and would drive home each weekend to see her (my friends still carrying out the exchange). I rented a tuxedo and met Kay at the school where the prom was happening. We had such a great time dancing, laughing, talking to friends—not realizing that a photographer was taking pictures. And yes, these pictures would appear in the school yearbook! When Kay's parents got the yearbook and saw us together, well, needless to say, it was time for me to get back to college and pretend like I was a good student.

As time passed, Kay's parents could see that we were not going to let each other go. They began to move slowly toward accepting me—still with great reservation. (Have you ever been around folks you know don't like you?)

I soon became bold enough to ask Kay to marry me, actually popping the question at a drive-in theater (I was such a romantic). I slipped this beautiful diamond ring on her finger when she was reaching for the popcorn (a hopeless romantic). This diamond was less than a quarter of a carat, but in Kay's eyes you'd have thought it was a 5 carat perfectly cut stone. It took Kay a while to tell her parents, and they were understandably disappointed but not shocked. They felt Kay deserved a much better person than me.

After a year at college, I came back home to Tulsa to take a job as a mail boy (yep, every morning up at 5am to the post office to get the mail) for an oil company. Six months later, I was called to active duty and stationed in Germany after spending 6 months in Communications / Intelligence School in Chicago. Kay's parents wanted her to spend one year in college, and then after that year, they agreed to fly her over to me so we could get married in Germany. What a show it was! Here she came with her two brothers, her dog, and her parents for the big day in Germany.

Due to German law, in order for our marriage to be legal, we had to be married at the courthouse with a German judge presiding. Then later that day, we had our formal wedding at the chapel on our base. Can you imagine being married twice in the same day? If you can remember your wedding day, men, how anxiety rushed through your veins, think about doing it twice. At the second ceremony, I was sweating so badly that I looked like I had just walked out of the shower.

Soon after we said our "I do's," her parents headed back to the states and left us to our happy life in Germany as Mr. and Mrs. Bob Goshen. Things went pretty well while I was in the service. We were sort of on a two-year honeymoon in Germany. I was in naval intelligence (I bet that makes you feel safe) and would work 6 days on and 4 days off. Sure, we would have our tiffs, but we made up quickly (the best part).

My two-year commitment overseas went by very quickly, and before long we were back in the states where reality set in. I was a young married man with no college education, no job contacts, driving a black 1971 Volkswagen Beetle (that means no air conditioning and a reserve fuel tank that you manually switched over when you were running out of gas . . . your basic stripped down piece of metal).

Kay and I decided we did not want to move in with either of our parents, so I immediately began looking for a job. Within two weeks, North American Rockwell hired me because of my military clearance. I was so proud; I had received a top secret cryptographic clearance in the Navy, and I just knew North American was going to move me straight to the top with those credentials. I went home and told Kay, "This is it baby; a job for life and I am headed for the top!" We celebrated over a glass of milk (all we could afford).

So the following Monday morning I showed up, and they said, "Let's jump in the golf cart and go out to the plant." On the way to the plant, we stopped by a clothing center where they issued me some navy blue khakis and steel-toed boots (should have given me some clue, but at that time in my life I would be what you consider clueless). Within an hour I found myself standing under the wing of a huge missile, a "hound dog missile," under which I would spend the next eight hours with a seven-pound electric sander over my head. I would sand the paint off a missile eight hours a day with a horn blowing every 50 minutes to give me a ten-minute break.

Now get this: I would strip the paint off the missile, repaint the missile, and then go out and hang it under the wing of a giant bomber called a B-52. Then they would fly the B-52 back to Vietnam where they would drop the missile and return for more missiles. Only the U.S. government would take two weeks painting a bomb destined to blow up!

Kay and I finally found a small garage apartment. Downstairs we had a kitchen and a couch, upstairs a bedroom, and the entire place was less than 800 square feet (you will never hear me say I wish we lived in the good old days). We had one little window air conditioner on the first floor, and there were so many nights in the August heat of Oklahoma when we would go downstairs with the mattress off our double bed and sleep on the floor next to the air conditioner to stay cool.

After about four weeks, I left North American (with 20inch biceps and my steel-toed boots) and went after a real job—yes a job that would set me on a career path in life—I became a forklift driver at Sears!

I want each of you to know that I would have been employee of the year for Sears except for the fact that I ran the forks of my forklift through the front of a stereo in the warehouse. Management failed to see the humor in that and immediately advanced me to delivery truck driver where I would spend every day delivering appliances to the low income areas of Tulsa.

I'm still amazed that people who were actually living in a shack would purchase a doublewide freezer/refrigerator. I can't count the number of times I would crawl under one of those shacks and reinforce the floor so that when we moved the refrigerator in, it wouldn't fall through to the ground underneath. We were constantly removing doors from their hinges and working for an hour to get those appliances installed. I know you will be very surprised when I say that it took me about three months to begin to observe that I was going nowhere in life (a sharper person would have caught on much faster).

So, there I was—no college, no job, and for the most part no real future. I would say this is when stress entered our marriage, and I became a "not-so-loving" husband. Kay and I decided that I should go back to college and walk on for a chance at a football scholarship, with the idea that Kay would find a job and we could make it work.

So within a month or two, off we went in our U-Haul truck (very small since we had very little hand-me-down furniture) with our beautiful black Volkswagen Beetle being towed behind. (Now hang with me—the story is about to get very colorful.)

We set up camp in a small home right behind the football stadium. Kay went to work at the telephone company, and I walked on in the football program at Oklahoma State University. Pretty soon, Kay decided to get pregnant. It was all her fault, like she didn't let me in on it as her husband. (Funny how everything is always the wife's fault.)

So now came the big game changer. I began to feel a little more pressure as a husband and father, and my high school love and companion wasn't so much fun anymore. That was about the time I decided college was a totally boring ordeal. I had only that one class I liked outside of football—that speech class I told you about. All the rest were worthless in my opinion.

After working my tail off to make the team, the coach called me in and said that I could come back the next year and expect a scholarship. Wow! What an exciting day!

And that is about as long as it lasted. The next day, that coach was fired and the new coach brought me in to say I had to begin all over again and come back next year to try out. My heart just fell out of my chest; I was under a lot of pressure with a new son, and financially we were just barely above water each month on our bills.

Kay was still working at the phone company, and I took a job at a company called Swan Rubber. I would work each night from 11pm until 7am the next morning.

All night long, I would operate a sky lift to move 100gallon drums of lead-wrapped hose into position. Each drum held several thousand feet of rubber hose (garden hose, air hose, etc.). The hose was encased in lead, and it was my job to pull the lead from the hose and lay the hose out in a figure eight—all night long. It was very hard labor, not to mention working with lead for eight hours each shift. Back in those days, no one mentioned things like lead poisoning. But I didn't complain since I had already developed 20-inch biceps from sanding the missiles we blew up over Vietnam.

Kay finally left her job at the telephone company and started her own business called "Goshen's Grooming," a dog grooming business and pet shop. She did very well, and she was and still is a hard worker—which I didn't appreciate at the time. Kay will do whatever it takes to make things work.

I would eventually leave the rubber company since eight hours of lead-stripping on top of my college schedule was overwhelming. I would come home, shower, and go to classes until 3pm, then suit up for football practice until around 6, go home, have dinner, go back to campus to watch films until 9, and then back to work at 11pm. I finally told Kay that I just couldn't continue. I knew I couldn't do it all, but I had to find a job to help support us. I found an advertisement in the paper for a salesman at a local office machine store. I didn't have much selling experience, but that day I sold the owner on the fact that he needed me.

It was a very difficult job to say the least. I had the job of selling typewriters and calculators to the college at Oklahoma State University. I did pretty well, and I soon discovered it was fun talking to people and sharing the latest in equipment. I loved to compete with other companies—the boys from IBM became my top target.

One day I found a desktop computer sitting in the corner of our company, very archaic related to today's standards but back then pretty cool. You used a magnetic strip card to create programs to run data. I asked the owner about it, and he said he didn't want to talk about it. He had sent two other salespeople to school to learn how to operate it, and both of them came back and quit; however, he allowed me to take the computer and the teaching manual home with me, and I began to teach myself how to use it. I came up with a set of programs that would add additional revenue to banks and lending organizations for installment notes. I determined to learn all I could about lending, and I developed the reputation of knowing how to solve mathematical problems related to banking equations. I became very tight with the Oklahoma Bankers Association and wrote programs that helped auditors check the math on loans made by banks in Oklahoma and Texas. I was on a base salary plus a commission, and the bucks began to roll in. However, the good news is the bad news. I spent five nights a week on the road, many times leaving the house on a Sunday night and returning late Friday night as I worked a four-state area.

When a spouse is gone that much, you lose track of time, and you actually forfeit your position as a husband and father—becoming virtually a stranger who appears once a week for 72 hours. (Do you see where this is going? I was getting ready to call a big meeting.)

I am not sure how it all happened, and I know it has happened to thousands of folks, but Kay and I began drifting apart. I left the parental duties to Kay while I was out on the road making a living; and friends, this is not a good place to be. I began to lose respect for Kay, using language around her that I had used around my Navy buddies. I began taking out all my stress on my dear wife, the one who wore that beautiful red dress, the one with the beautiful green eyes that glistened in the sun; that same woman was now receiving my wrath—all underserved. I would put her down making her feel less than a woman. I began going out with the boys drinking and staying out late, while she took our son with her to work each day and slaved grooming dogs.

We came so close to calling it quits after our first seven years. A gentleman who sold insurance became friends with my wife, and he would come over and listen to Kay. He was doing what I should have been doing, and after a few months he asked my wife to leave me and join him. I have been asked on occasion if I didn't want to go after him, but I know it was not his fault. If I had been the husband and father God required me to be (even though I didn't know Christ at the time), I would never have allowed that door to open. Gentlemen, please listen when I say that if you do not love your lady, someone is waiting to do that for you. Within just seven years, I had turned a lady who worshiped me and loved me into a person that actually . . . her words . . . "hated my guts." I am confident at this point in our story that many of you ladies can identify — perhaps you're at the point Kay was when she "hated me." And perhaps some of you men are facing the same struggles with your wives.

Then a miracle occurred: a couple came to the pet shop, developed a friendship with Kay, and shared with her the gospel of Jesus Christ. Kay, even though she attended church her entire life, had never had a personal relationship with Christ. God had pre-planned this day for Kay to become a new creation in Christ, and she began growing in her faith. At the same time, I am still the terrible husband and father traveling five days a week. Soon after that, another miracle would occur: we would sell the pet shop (totally God's provision), and within a couple more weeks, I would have a major disagreement with my business partner and would sell him my share of the business. I decided to move back to Tulsa and begin my own office equipment company.

To save time and move toward the point of this chapter, let's just say I became worse as a husband and father while Kay was learning the meaning of the **I** in **GRIP**—she was learning to **initiate her faith**. I criticized her faith, refused to have anything to do with it, would not go to church, was very vocal—filthy vocal—at times. And this is where the story can only get better!

# 8

# WHEN THE HOLY SPIRIT
# VISITS THE GOSHEN HOME

Kay became sensitive to the Holy Spirit and quit working on me as God showed her that she was to hand me over to Him and work on her personal relationship with Him. When Kay was doing her morning Bible study (naturally I was gone since she was fearful of opening the Bible around me), she opened the Bible to 1 Peter 3:1-2 which reads:

> *In the same way, you wives must accept the authority of your husbands. Then, even if some refuse to obey the Good News, your godly lives will speak to them without any words. They will be won over by observing your pure and reverent lives.*

This scripture confirmed that her godly life was more important than trying to make me conform. A big step for Kay! Think about it: she had accepted Christ 18 months earlier and had to live with a godless husband and father during all this time, yet she stayed faithful to the Word of God. Now let me share a quick side note. I do believe that God honored her through His word. But ladies, do not allow this scripture to hold you in a relationship that is physically abusive. If your man is physically harming you, leave. And if you have children, take them with you.

I am not saying divorce; I am saying separate first if at all possible. Do not stay if you are being used as a punching bag. And if any man reading this is physically harming his wife, you need help now!

## Breaking Down Kay's Bible Verse

In I Peter 3:1-2, the verses Kay claimed prior to my conversion, I have to focus on a portion of this verse that was crucial in my personal salvation.

> *In the same way, you wives must accept the authority of your husbands. Then, even if some refuse to obey the Good News,* [get ready for this next sentence ladies] ***your godly lives will speak to them without any words. They will be won over by observing your pure and reverent lives.***

My dear ladies, if your life mirrors your husband's poor choices—you are using profane language, going out for a drink with your friends, or you are dressing to impress other men—that is not a godly life.

Ladies, if you are continually attacking your husband verbally, telling him about all his faults or comparing him with another man, this is not godly. Ladies, if you spend more time in a sexually graphic novel than in the Bible, this is not pure and reverent behavior. My point is simple but straightforward. You can't have one foot in the world while preaching the Bible to your lost husband. The question remains: does he see a godly wife; does he see a pure and reverent woman?

I was a very lost man . . . out of control with my language and my actions. During the 18 months Kay had to live with me as an unsaved man, she never at any time said

"You need to be taking me and our kids to church;" "You need to be like Larry at our church who loves Jesus;" "You need to open your Bible and read it."

She never raised her voice; she went out of her way not to force religion on me or force me to attend the church she was attending. My darling wife exhibited the attributes of a godly wife, and I began to observe her pure and reverent life.

I am very confident that the demons of Hell hated how my wife submitted to Jesus and His Word, and in everything she was doing she was doing it "unto the Lord" and not "unto Bob Goshen." She never opened the Bible and read it in front of me; she never voiced her prayers in front of me, and for sure she did not run down the street and tell her friends how bad Bobby was as a husband and father. As much as I believe it is important for us to pray with one another, I must warn you ladies not to share your husband's bad traits and the details of your marriage at your weekly Bible study. I wish everyone in your circle was a believer, but unfortunately many are not, and they can't wait to share your problems with their friends and their husbands— which in time will come back to your husband.

For 18 months, my wife believed God directed her to stop praying for **me** and to begin praying for **herself**, to ask God to make her the wife and mother He desired her to be and to hand me over to God and allow Him to work through others and His Spirit to penetrate my heart.

Kay was exercising the **P—Prayer**—in our **GRIP** acronym long before either of us fully understood that **God is sovereign**, that we should **rejoice** in our circumstances, **initiate our faith**, and **pray** through the tunnels we would encounter.

I know many fine ladies are reading these words, and I feel it is my responsibility to share what a non-believer saw in a believer—a godly wife who gave it all to Christ. So ask yourself, are you that vessel God can use; are you the pure and reverent lady described in 1 Peter 3:1-2; are you willing to give your mate up to God and focus on refining your own relationship with Him?

## The Great Fall

1975 was the year of **the great fall**. That was the year my business and my life fell apart. The company that I had worked so hard to create was going under, my marriage was falling apart, my relationship with my kids was horrible, I was spending more time out on the town drinking with the boys, and I could see that I was losing everything. Not just financially but emotionally. Go back and read the verse Kay was given, and you will understand how the Holy Spirit began to stir my heart and soul.

I still remember coming home that night around midnight, my usual time. Kay and the kids were in bed, and I went straight to the living room, dropped down on my knees and said this simple prayer: "God, I am so tired, so very tired. You know where I am. I ask that you take total control over my life and show me wisdom for becoming a

BOB GOSHEN

better man, husband, and father. Forgive me of my many sins." That was it. No lightning strikes, no thunder in the sky, no visible signs flashing in heaven, just those words and off to bed I went. My friends, that was the **great fall,** when heaven fell on me on that September evening. I did not share anything with Kay for several weeks, but she noticed some visible signs—no more filthy language, no more verbal put-downs, no more exploding responses, no more yelling and making demands. I poured out my liquor cabinet and quit a 17-year habit of smoking.

I couldn't get enough of the Bible. I went to Bible studies and even spent two semesters at a Bible college. I wanted to learn about how so many religions and church denominations were created from the time Christ was taken off the cross until the 20th century.

I remember the day I went to the admissions office to ask if they had such a course. The young lady said, "Well, we have a course that would address that, but what is your major?" I didn't have a major, and I wasn't interested in college credit. I just wanted truth. She was so apologetic, and she had a hard time understanding why I didn't have a problem paying for a course with no apparent benefit.

So three days a week for two hours a day I attended a class where a tender, partially blind, 80-year-old man took us through the Scriptures and early church history. His spirit was so kind, his words so gentle, and each word resonated with truth.

126

At the same time God began to put godly men in my life; it was such a confirmation. For the first time, I attended what the Southern Baptists call a "revival." I still have the notes in my Bible from this pastor who was like the early Billy Sunday. (Billy Sunday, a famous preacher in the late 1800's to early 1900's, was what is often referred to as a "hellfire and brimstone preacher." He was loud and let you know there was a heaven and there was a hell.) The evangelist preached on "spiritual warfare," heaven and hell, God's sovereignty, Nicodemus meeting Jesus. . . . I was so excited! I would get home around 10pm, go into the bedroom, and begin teaching Kay what I had learned. I was a complete sponge.

Then God led us to a church where the pastor taught word-for-word, verse-by-verse through the Bible. He was so clear, and I marked up my Bible from front to back and top to bottom with notes from his sermons.

Then God sent a visiting pastor to the church. He was from England; his name was John Blanchard, and the pastor asked if Kay and I would let him stay at our home. Wow! God used that man to teach me one-on-one—again teaching how God was sovereign and in total control. He took me to Psalm 139 and opened my eyes to the truth that I was special to God. He took me to a Christian bookstore and purchased books written by Charles Haddon Spurgeon and Arthur Pink, and historical books about the reformation. I couldn't get enough. I felt like the proverbial baby bird— "feed me, feed me." I was actually experiencing becoming "a new creation in Christ—all things becoming new." It was like a rain on my soul: Tom Elliff, Ruffin Snow, and Ralph Speas, man after man coming as mentors sharing truth.

While this was going on, I was praying for an opportunity to keep my family alive financially. My beautiful wife was so strong during this time. She allowed me time to grow even though she was almost two years ahead of me in understanding the Bible. She would sit there hour after hour just listening to me, never interrupting as I poured out what I was learning. Even as life was beginning to look pretty bleak on the financial front, she was focused on her faith that God would supply our needs.

Within the same month that I became a Christ-follower, I learned about another business opportunity. The evangelist who introduced me to Christ introduced me to a businessman who was part of his evangelical association, and this gentleman showed us a way we could save ourselves financially if we were willing to work. I agreed, and within three years Kay and I were financially blessed beyond any human wisdom.

Thank you for reading this story. It is so much a part of who we are that I wanted to share as much as I could without losing your interest.

### Lessons Learned in the Marriage Tunnel

So let's look at what I had created during the early years of my marriage and how "I called the meeting" that made our marriage terrible for the first seven years. Please don't feel that I'm "talking down" to you; I simply wish to review the many mistakes I made, tell you how I corrected those mistakes, and share with you how God stands ready to renew your marriage once you bow to His authority.

First, my wife and I did not have a personal relationship with Christ when we married. So as I reflect on my actions as a husband, I see that I exhibited the same actions my father exhibited as a husband and father.

I was explosive; I was always right; Kay was stupid, and I was smarter, and if anything went wrong in the home, it was Kay's fault. I would always find ways to put Kay down with my words. I had a little child's attitude in a grown man's body.

Some of you gentlemen reading this at this moment exhibit these same attributes, and sadly some reading these words are even men that profess to be Christians. Gentlemen, whether you are a believer in Christ or not, a man should never treat his mate in the manner in which I treated Kay for the first seven years.

As husbands and leaders of our homes, we need to be conscious of what God reveals in His Word about the husband/wife relationship and answered prayer. I cannot tell you the number of times I have visited with Christian men who told me that their lives are headed in the wrong direction and they feel that God is not hearing their prayers. I believe that the way you treat your wife has a lot to do with whether your prayer life is active or on hold. Later in the passage that directed Kay's life, Paul talks to us husbands:

*"In the same way, you husbands must give honor to your wives. Treat your wife with understanding as you live together. She may be weaker than you are, but she is your equal partner in God's gift of new life. Treat her as you should so your **prayers will not be hindered.**" (1 Peter 3:7)*

So gentlemen, many Christian husbands who are not honoring their wives are having their prayers hindered. This verse jumped out at me early in my spiritual life. In simple Aggie English: treat your wife poorly—expect nothing from your prayers.

In addition, if you have a son, he needs to see you exhibiting understanding and honoring love for your wife so when he marries, he will treat his wife like he saw his father treating his mother. If you happen to be one of those men who is a walking tyrant—always in a rant and putting down your wife and being verbally abusive—it's pretty certain your son will do the same.

You might just say, "Well, it is what it is," but let's say you also have a daughter you feel is just precious and can do no wrong. How are you going to respond when she marries a young man just like you, and he begins to treat your daughter like you treat your wife? Think through that scenario, for as fathers we are setting the stage for our children, and they will act out and accept what they see us doing. How would you feel knowing your wonderful daughter is being treated like "hell" by some man who can only pick on the weaker vessel? You see gentlemen, we are grooming young men who will be marrying young ladies, and how those young men see us behaving creates habits they will live out.

Let's look at another example. My children are grown and in their late 30's. The other day, one of my children told some people that they had never seen me and Kay argue or fight during all their years at home. Have you ever heard someone say, "Arguing makes a marriage stronger and shows the children the real world of marriage"? I'd say those folks have never understood how to treat each other in marriage. Now to say that Kay and I did not have differences would be wrong, but when we did have these "discussions," we always made sure they happened out of the children's presence. You ask why? Well, we both came from families characterized by continual fighting, putdowns, and shallow threats.

As a result, whenever we disagreed, we both flashed back to our youth and how we felt when we witnessed our parents in such an outrage. And we both remembered how insecure we felt. You see, when you are young, your parents are your only security. If they openly demonstrate their hostility to one another and use the "D" word (divorce), the kids become very insecure and their behavior reveals that. Often these kids fall behind in school as they see their world falling apart. They often begin believing it is "their fault" that mom and dad are fighting. And when parents divorce, it is often the child who feels the greatest pain.

Sure, we have all heard people say, "We had a very easy divorce with no stress," or "We actually spend more quality time with our kids now that we are divorced," but friends, you are sending signals to your children that can alter their lives dramatically.

We ask ourselves today why there are so many divorces. Could it be that so many children have witnessed their parents' divorces so "it's natural to do it"? We send the signal to young men that not living up to a commitment is fine and that wedding vows are meaningless in "the real world."

I was so fortunate to have my children when I was very young—when I was not functioning as a real husband and father. So for the majority of their lives, they have witnessed a man who loves their mother and cherishes her.

So let's talk about divorce. Listen, I realize many reading this have gone through that experience, and many reading this are in the middle of a divorce or contemplating a divorce. My lovely wife says it this way: "Life is like a game of golf; you must hit the ball from where it lies." So if you are divorced, move forward in life. But as you move forward, look back and face why the divorce occurred. I wish a divorce could be one-sided, but it generally does require two people. When I was considering divorce, two very selfish people were involved. You see, Kay and I have discussed how close we came to divorce in those early days, and we both agree we had the "I" attitude—"I want this, I want that, I deserve this, I do not deserve that." It's so typical in the society we have created. We are the "me generation." It's all about ME! But when Kay and I, through God's amazing grace, came back together, it was all about "them." It was all about serving one another, giving to one another, preferring one another. When we took our selfish attitudes out of the mix, the marriage began to heal.

Let's be very clear: marriage demands and requires work. You work to make a great marriage, you focus on the needs of the other person, and you work to make sure your words to your mate are uplifting and edifying. You make the decision that it will no longer be "all about me," —my desires, my needs, my wishes. You determine that by God's grace and through God's power you will love and serve one another.

.

# 9

# WHAT WOMEN DESIRE

I am not a psychologist, but after 47 years of marriage I do feel I have earned a PhD on the subject of marriage. I feel I know what the majority of women desire in a man, and I will reveal my beliefs:

Over the years, our culture has promoted a major attack on what I call "manhood." The great "women's liberation movement" has created very weak men.

Men no longer know what women desire and need in order to thrive as women, wives, and mothers. Now hear me out, since I have two daughters and now 5 granddaughters, I am all for all these ladies having the same rights as men in the workplace and beyond. I want all my girls to dream big dreams and equip themselves to achieve these dreams. But I also want the men in their lives to become the men God intended them to be, not men of this world. I feel confident about what I have learned after 47 years in my own marriage and after observing what my parents created—a "home of hell" rather than a "home of heaven." I think my personal observations can give guidance to all men, so listen up and here we go!

Men, God has called us to be the **priest**, the **provider**, and the **protector**. Guess what? This is precisely what every woman is looking for in a man, a man that will guide them spiritually, provide for them financially, and protect them physically and emotionally. Am I on track, ladies?

## Priest

Pray for your ladies every day. Lift them up to God that they will have the wisdom needed to raise your children or make the decisions necessary to succeed at work. Pray for their health; pray the blessings of Christ over them as they sleep each night. Ask God to make you the man He requires you to be in order to be the husband and father who can minister to the woman who is putting her trust in you as a leader. A priest is careful with his words—words that are uplifting and encouraging, words that make her feel completed as a woman. A priest opens the Bible and shares the word with his mate, and he lets her know that her input from God's Word is vitally important to his fulfillment as the priest of the home.

As priests we are to guard the environment of our ladies. We are to be observant to what is around them and the language others use in their presence. A priest ensures that his mate can confide in him and share her fears. Gentlemen, the Word of God is very clear that our prayers will be answered or hindered based upon our care for our ladies.

A priest is conscious that the fellowship of other believers is vitally important for reinforcing his belief in God and His ways. Finding a strong church home is important for both you and your mate.

## Provider

This is a touchy subject today since both husband and wife typically work. Over the past four decades, I have found that most families have put themselves under such dire financial conditions that they seem to believe they must both work. But in all fairness, the majority of us work because of our endless desire to have more and more things. We must have two cars, multiple cell phones, wardrobes that are hip, more restaurant meals than at-home meals. And we have fallen into the "must ensure that my kids have everything they want" trap. Then we naturally feel we must pay for our kid's college (for goodness sake we don't want them to have to work while they are in college). Because we are stuck on this crazy treadmill, our wives have to work, and many of us have to have two jobs. We feel that it is our duty as parents to keep this constant financial spiral moving.

Now, once again hear me out. I have no problem whatsoever with a wife working if she feels the need, but what I am saying is that God did not call her to be the provider. He called **us**, men! We need to take control of our finances in such a way that our ladies don't need to work unless they want to. You see, God has placed this internal calling on the man to provide for his woman. It is driven by God's Spirit, and it actually fulfills the man when he can provide for his family on his own. Now, in the same breath I will tell you that because of the way we have raised many of our sons today, these young boys have fallen into the "entitlement mentality" believing that their wives need to step up and help them.

And when we give our kids everything they desire, they will expect that from their boss, their business partner, and their marriage partner. Gentlemen, as my good friend Tom Kelley would say, it is time to "cowboy up," take the reins of your home, and be the provider.

## Protector

When we think of protection, our first thought is physical protection—certainly needed. We need to be observant of our ladies at all times because, as men, we know how other men (especially those who are godless) view women. Pornography has taken center stage today. I have always heard that you become what you focus on and what you fill your mind with. I also believe that women are more naïve and trusting than men. They often are not aware of what is going on around them and what men are thinking. So yes, we must be prepared to physically protect our ladies.

But we also need to protect our ladies in what enters their minds though our vocabulary. There was a time in my life when I could embarrass a drunken sailor with my language. And before we knew Christ, Kay and I were often around other couples whose language became very filthy. But guys, there's no reason to use the "f-bombs" around our wives or use language that denigrates others and shows our personal ignorance. You might say, "Bob, you need to get in touch with the real world!" To which I would respond, "My friends, take a look at the real world and ask yourself,

'How's it working out for everyone?'" How do you feel living in a home filled with negativity? How do you feel when your friends use vulgar language around your wife? Have you accepted so much that you are no longer sensitive to your words?

Protection for me is also making sure that what comes into my home through music, television, and movies will build up and edify my wife. My kids can attest to the fact that we have walked out of many movies and asked for our money back due to language or sexual content. Again, some of you say, "Bob you need to get over it!" To which I am going to say "**Nope**!" I am not going to give in to this world of pornography, filthy language, and disrespect portrayed in film or on TV. I am not interesting in hearing someone sing songs filled with violence, hate, or filthy language around my wife or anyone else.

I also believe I am to protect how my wife dresses and looks. "Oh my goodness Bob, you sound so old fashioned!" Gentlemen, I dress for only one person, my wife; and my wife dresses for only one person, me. I am not married to a runway model or a half-clothed woman modeling for Victoria's Secret. Kay and I are very modern and contemporary in our wardrobe . . . and fashionable but not **provocative**. Gentlemen, don't be afraid to step up and tell your wife if you feel her wardrobe is a little "over the top." And ladies, please don't get emotional over this issue. Your husband **should** have an opinion about the way he wants you to look and dress. And hopefully, it isn't like "a lady of the night." Now please hear me out on this, I am talking to believers on these issues—not unbelievers. Ladies, if your daddy didn't teach you, I will. Men are inspired by sight, and women are inspired by touch. Men receive messages based upon how you are dressed, and their reply is often "I want some of that." Once Kay and I became one in marriage and one in Christ, we no longer needed to impress our friends and others of the opposite sex like we did as singles.

Christian mothers, how you dress is a model for your daughters. So ladies, remember you are being observed, and one of the worst conversations you will ever have with your daughter is when you correct her and she says "But mom, you do it!"

Ladies, pornography on the internet is rampant. The men and boys who are addicted to it are more inclined to say and do things they otherwise would never say or do.

Folks, I am no better than anyone reading this book; as a matter of fact I'm like the Apostle Paul who said he was the chief sinner. But I have made the choice to support positive, uplifting values. After 40 years of mentoring people around the world—from top CEO's to pastors, husbands, wives, and young adults—I know what works and what leads to successful relationships.

### Trust/Trustworthiness

Men, as leaders of our homes and wives, we must each day show ourselves trustworthy in order to earn trust from our ladies. Trust goes both ways, but here are just a few obvious and maybe not so obvious ways you can violate the trust of your wife:

- Saying you are going to do something for her and then not doing it.
- Saying you are going to be at a certain place at a certain time and constantly being late.
- Sharing together your ideas and dreams and never following through.
- Spending more time with your man friends than with your wife.
- Putting your needs and desires before hers.
- Failing to follow through on your commitments.
- Putting her in harm's way with bad people who use bad language.
- Facebooking or emailing old girlfriends or any lady of the opposite sex without her knowledge.

Marriage is based on trust and trustworthiness; it is one of the cornerstones for a successful, solid marriage. Each day I have to show myself trustworthy to Kay in order for Kay to trust me. This is reciprocal, for each day Kay must show herself trustworthy so I can trust her. Men, you thought once you were married that all you needed to do was put your marriage on cruise control and drift through life, huh? But you see, a good marriage requires constant work that comes from a servant's heart for your mate; it is often challenging but very rewarding.

## Living It

Wow! News Flash! Now it's time for me to heed my own teaching and get a **GRIP**. Yesterday I was informed that my son-in-law is divorcing my daughter. So while I am writing this book, I am entering another tunnel . . . one which I never imagined I would be entering.

They have been married for over 15 years; they have two great children, a nice home, a good income, and by most standards they are living the ideal. Sure, they have had their marital arguments and differences over the years, but none that would drive them to this place. In a very calm matter-of-fact way, my son-in-law sat down with my daughter two days ago and said "I'm just not happy." As I have already said, all divorce springs from a selfish heart; the big "I" says "I want this," "I expect this," "I deserve this." It is always about someone's personal desires rather than God's desire for that person. So here I go into the tunnel of divorce as a father and grandfather.

I can't really describe my initial emotions—shock, sadness, dislike for my son-in-law, sorrow for my grandchildren, fear for my daughter's emotional wellbeing. But quickly I had to leave the emotional, the normal and natural feelings, and move toward spiritual answers. Yes, your author who has been mentoring you through the past several chapters had to personally get a **GRIP**.

I had to overcome my emotions and shift back to what I teach knowing that even during this time of hurt for our family, **God is sovereign**, and I respect the truth that He is in control of this tunnel full of challenges.

Second, I refuse to become bitter and give the demons of Hell the opportunity to dwarf my spiritual life and draw me back into natural worldly thoughts, so I began to and continue to **rejoice** during this time—not for the divorce but through it, giving my spirit an opportunity to line up with the Holy Spirit. I am **initiating my faith**, believing that my son-in-law's heart can be changed, and believing that a sovereign God does control his heart, just as he does mine. And finally, I will continue to break open the Book of Life and **pray** that our God in Heaven will give me the wisdom needed to work through this new tunnel.

"Dear God give me the wisdom to respond to my daughter, my grandchildren, and my son-in-law. I pray for salvation for those who are in need and restoration for this family. I pray that You will lead other believers to share with my son-in-law, just as God did for me during my time of struggle. I pray that my daughter and grandchildren will be protected spiritually and will search God's Word during this time of trial. I pray for wisdom on the practical side should this continue to a final divorce decree—that I will be wise in assisting my daughter to seek proper counsel, that she will be protected financially, and I pray for the wellbeing of my grandchildren."

Folks, I can tell you it hurts, it especially hurts to see my grandchildren crying and asking "Why?" The ripple effect on the entire family and our friends continues to spread.

I have been asked to pray for people who have gone through this challenge, and I have. But honestly, only when you are actually going through the same battle do you understand the many ramifications and emotions. I know at this very moment there are hundreds if not thousands reading this book who are where I am today, and I feel more strongly than ever that unless you acknowledge God as the hand that will lead you through this tunnel, the tunnel can become extremely dark.

I also can say, without Christ at the center of a marriage, that marriage is destined for destruction or hardship. As I focus on our challenge, I also recognize that sometimes it happens in the opposite way . . . where the wife abandons her husband and children. It matters not who left or even how they left, but only that they have now decided to forsake the commitment made before God and man on that wedding day.

I am amazed at the negative opinions and advice many people have offered to us and to our daughter. It makes me flash back to the book of Job where his friends (so called) came around him to offer all the reasons for his challenges.

So many have said she will be "better off," or that "he was a bum to begin with." Some might say "Why would God do this?" On and on the comments come. Yet here is what we must all realize: the sin nature of man and woman create this—divorce is never something that just happens overnight. There are weeks if not months where one party begins thinking about the possibility . . . considering taking that tunnel . . . calling the meeting.

There are many yellow lights you and your mate run through before you finally run the red one. Yes, I have found that each party runs the yellow lights; it is never one-sided.

Yes, it is true . . . God hates divorce. Malachi 2:16

> "For I hate divorce!" says the LORD the God of Israel. "To divorce your wife is to overwhelm her with cruelty," says the LORD of Heaven's Armies. "So guard your heart; do not be unfaithful to your wife."

Divorce is **not** from God, but God has given men and women the ability to make choices. For the first seven years of my marriage, all my choices were based upon the world and the great counsel of my drinking buddies. Praise God, the Spirit of God quickened my spirit (no man can come to God unless he is drawn by the Spirit) and my choices changed from worldly to godly choices.

### Forgiveness

Wow, this is tough! I wish I could just fall on my spiritual knees and say that I am such a godly man that I have no bad thoughts toward my son-in-law, but the human side of me screams negative thoughts. Yet the Word is clear that my daughter, I, my wife, and all those who are close to my daughter must exercise forgiveness and give this to God.

Remember the **R** in grip? Rejoice? This is not rejoicing for what happened but rejoicing through what is happening. Relationships often produce hurt and the need to forgive. The forgiving is for our souls and our spirits so they can begin to align with God's Word.

> *"Get rid of all bitterness, rage, anger, harsh words, and slander, as well as all types of evil behavior. Instead, be kind to each other, tenderhearted, forgiving one another, just as God through Christ has forgiven you."* (Ephesians 4:31-32)

Ouch! There are times when I read words in the Bible I wish I had not read, and this is one of those times. But as believers we must turn this over to God, work through the proper legal process, and begin to forgive. Again, we choose to rejoice saying, "God I hate this; my stomach turns as I go through this; I feel wronged, but I know that you want me to become stronger as your follower during this time. To do this means to follow your words. God, it is not natural, but I will step into the unnatural in living faith as I go through this difficult tunnel."

Folks, a forgiving heart is one that can move forward, a heart that is open to God's Spirit, a heart that is obedient to God, and a heart in which God can produce great peace. When we choose a rejoicing and forgiving spirit, we shed the feelings that create anger and stress, and in their place we experience only sorrow for the person and the actions that have hurt us.

Because of my son-in-law's action and my immediate desire to protect my daughter, it would be easy to set my son-in-law up as my enemy and my daughter's enemy. This would be the natural way men and women (fathers and mothers) navigate the challenges of divorce. But this morning during my daily Bible reading, God had a scripture ready for me:

> *"But to you who are willing to listen, I say, love your enemies! Do good to those who hate you. Bless those who curse you. Pray for those who hurt you." (Luke 6:27-28)*

Did you really notice how Luke began? *". . to you who are **willing to listen**. . . ."* It is like he was saying to me: *"Bob, if you are willing to listen to the truth, I can help you during this time."* Think about it; He knew His words would be a hard pill to swallow for the majority of people, and He also knew only a few would listen.

This defines the way I am to respond as I move forward. Be firm in allowing the law to function for my daughter and grandchildren but work diligently to refuse to see this through the eyes of hate and anger and carry on through eyes of sorrow. God is the judge in all of this—not me—so it is my responsibility to allow God to work through me during this time of trial.

I am more than confident that God will lead our entire family though this uncharted water of divorce and hurt. God and only God is the master teacher, and this is a time for me to dig deeper in my soul and find forgiveness as I seek His will and His wisdom moving forward.

To you who are reading this from the entrance to the tunnel of divorce, from the middle of it, or from its end, let us be tender to the teachings of the Holy Spirit and let this time become a great time for God's Word to educate us as we begin a new direction. Wherever you are in the process, please let it be known that now I understand and I have added the following my daily prayer life:

*"Lord God, bless those who are navigating the tunnel called divorce. Let their hearts not be lonely and fearful but full of You, Your love, and Your wisdom. Help them to let go of words, thoughts, and actions that can undermine their spiritual life, but give them words to lift their spirits closer to your Spirit. Amen."*

# 10

# MORE DRUGS & ALCOHOL

It is apparent "the enemy" does not want me to finish this book; he is working diligently to make me stop writing and direct my energy to fight his onslaught. As I just shared in the earlier chapter, my son-in law has initiated an action to divorce my daughter, which immediately plunged me into living the words I've been sharing in this book.

Last week our son's wife phoned and told us that our son was in the emergency room having fainted at work. We knew that he had relapsed with his use of alcohol, and once again we had more or less just left him on his own journey to figure it out while we prayed many times throughout the day and night that God would intervene if it would be His will.

We hadn't visited with our son for the past six months, and there we were at his bedside in the ER. He was having trouble breathing and was very weak. A cardiologist was assigned to him, and in short order they determined he had a heart arrhythmia, the heart having difficulty sustaining a normal rhythm. They rushed him into the operating room and performed a procedure where they run a wire to the heart and shock it back into rhythm. Fortunately it worked; but as a result, the cardiologist determined that my son's heart was only functioning at 20%. The years of alcohol and hard living had actually taken away 80% of his heart function. The doctor was very up-front telling Rob that if he continues drinking, he cannot avoid certain death. Folks, alcohol is terminal; it is just a matter of time.

So, if you are in this tunnel or have family in this tunnel, here we are again—totally with you—as we fall back together, get a **GRIP**, and move forward.

The realities of alcohol have surrounded me throughout my entire life. My father was an alcoholic and my son is an alcoholic, so I have witnessed firsthand the realities of this disease. Many of you reading this book are in this battle at this very moment—many parents are watching their children fade deeper and deeper into the clutches of this disease, and many of you have a husband, wife, or other loved one who is under this attack. I've spent many years researching this disease, traveled thousands of miles to talk to doctors and counselors who treat its victims, and I have heard all the theories of its origins—inheriting it, forming bad habits, or hanging out with the wrong people. I've attended conferences listening to speakers contradict themselves with their findings and debate over who is right and wrong. After observing my father's journey and witnessing my son's tunnel, I have my own personal conclusion: **no one can stop the behavior without intervention.** I do not mean the intervention of a facility or family but the intervention of the Almighty God. The hours I have spent studying the topic lead me to the belief that until the person surrenders his spirit to God, repents, and begins to seek to follow Christ, he or she will never be free from this terminal disease.

As I've sought answers to the complexities of alcoholism, God has placed many significant people in my life who have been redeemed from this disease—folks who were heavily addicted and have been set free from addiction. They each share their story of how when God steps in, the addiction steps out. These men are all my personal friends, and I see them often throughout the year, each time witnessing their personal growth in Christ.

## Tony's Story

It was 1999. I was living in NYC, and I just came off a week of drinking and drugs and I felt so defeated. I remember walking into a Catholic church, and I needed help. I was looking for answers. I waited in line to go into a confession booth. I finally got inside and told the priest I had been drinking and using drugs nonstop for the last week, I couldn't seem to stop, and I needed help. He turned to me and said, "Son, I understand. I can help you. Please wait for me in the pew, and when I am finished there is somewhere I want to take you." As we were leaving the church, he told me that he was an alcoholic, too, and he was taking me to a 12-step program. That was the first time I heard that you needed to have a higher power or you would never stop drinking or using drugs. I had an idea of God but had no idea about having a real relationship with God. I left that meeting thinking I was now on my way to recovery, but the reality was that was the furthest thing from the truth.

My vicious addiction cycle continued along with all the cover-ups and lies. I always seemed to run off people in my life; whether it was through verbal abuse, manipulation, or being a flat out bully. My denial was in full force. I had this black hole inside of me that seemed like the size of Texas that could never be satisfied. It was always about me and how I felt.

This cycle was repeated in my life every couple months. I was what they call a functioning alcoholic. This type wastes so much time trying to keep it hidden from the world and doing their best to pretend they are sober. Ten years of doing this behavior is exhausting as it is lie upon lie upon lie to keep the story going. My cycle looked like this: I would disappear for three days and no one would know where I was. I would isolate myself and have no communication with anyone. I would drink to escape the loneliness I constantly felt in my life even though I was the life of the party. I tried to fill that black hole with everything from booze, drugs, food, women, and making money. I even thought that if I just got married that things would get better. I was the guy that brushed everything under the rug and never dealt face-to-face with anything. Like it would magically go away and everything was fine. After those three days, I would have overwhelming guilt and shame. I always said at the time that I needed help and I promised I would never drink or do drugs again. I would be "OK" in my terms for a couple weeks, and then the behaviors would start sneaking in before the next cycle started. Every good thing God brought into my life I would find a way to completely sabotage it.

With ten years of my addiction being out of control, I have had five near-death experiences. Even with my last near-death experience in 2004, it would take me six long years later to fully surrender to God.

It started out that day with some social drinks with friends. It quickly moved to bars and then at night a hotel party. I got to the hotel party but have no idea how I actually got there. There were a lot of people, drugs, and booze there. I remember myself walking out to the balcony. Next thing I know, I had fallen three stories to the cement. I landed on the left side of my body — thank God — and not my head which would have been crushed. I remember coming in and out of consciousness and the paramedics being over me. They carried me on a gurney and into the ambulance. The next time I awoke was in the hospital room. I was in ICU with all kinds of machines hooked up to me. I would later find out that I had internal bleeding and different parts of my organs were shutting down. I also shattered my left radius bone and elbow, had a punctured lung, and broken ribs. Needless to say, I was fighting for my life.

I was lying there all alone. My friends from that party were nowhere to be found. My family was 3,000 miles away, and no one knew I was lying there. I started thinking about my life. It wasn't about Tony being the "cool party guy," or being defined by the money I made, where I lived or all the things I thought were important. I thought about if I died right now, what was my legacy? What would people remember me by? My wild booze nights, the horrible way I treated people to get what I wanted, the way money controlled every move I made, how everything was about Tony? What would it be? I had no wife, no kids . . . no real purpose to serve others.

I had this imaginary vision that when I died, all these amazing friends and family would surround me. They would be sharing stories of my extraordinary life and how many things I had done for others, my community, and my family. As I lay there, I quickly realized none of that at this very moment was the truth. I said to myself, when I get out of here, I do not want to be the same man ever again. I will create the life I always wanted. Problem with that is that God already had a plan for me and all I needed to do was trust Him and follow the plan. But, again I thought I knew better and I would create my own destiny.

I found a church that I started going to and told myself going to church every Sunday and being there counted as recovery. It didn't. I would go but really I was just a shell there. I was still tormented by the addiction. I thought by showing up, magically the addiction would go away.

I was still so badly trying to fill that black hole. I got married and thought that was the ticket. Now that I was married, I had to get strategic. I would make sure I could travel for work, and in those other cities I would binge for days. I thought I was smart. I was crushing my wife. There were times she had no idea where I was and I was 2,500 miles away. After two years of marriage, we found ourselves in marriage counseling. My wife basically gave me an ultimatum. Even in counseling, I thought I could fool our therapist. I would say all the right things and the minute I was back in my car I reverted back.

My whole life was crumbling around me once again. My ten years of a façade was falling apart. My parents, my wife's parents, and everyone else now knew what was really going on. My so-called identity was gone, and the alcoholic was fully present for everyone to see. I was going to lose my wife and probably die from an overdose. Everything finally came to a screeching halt.

I literally got on my knees and cried like a baby. For the very first time, I fully surrendered to God. I prayed he would take this craving away for good. God answers prayers as He did just that! The craving to this day has never come back. That is when I truly believed He could take the impossible and make it possible! I also knew I needed a relationship with Him, but my whole life I ran from building intimate relationships. I needed His help to give me wisdom and guidance in building a "real" relationship with Him. That day was May 13, 2010.

As I write this, I am three weeks short of four years of sobriety. Today, my life is nothing short of a miracle and God's grace over me. I have learned that God is a BIG and understanding God—He's got my back. I don't need to worry about every little thing. Worrying means I don't trust God. I was looking for peace everywhere else except with Him. I now take peace over anything else. I realize that without God, I make bad decisions and hurt people. I have learned to lean on Him and love unconditionally. Before I open my mouth, react or do anything, I ask myself "What would Jesus do in this situation? How would Jesus handle this?" I have learned to make good decisions through Him.

I have also realized that it is about having a relationship with God, not about a religion. Repeating words or phrases while at mass meant nothing. Having a real conversation with God every day meant everything!

It is so true that your message is in your mess. I feel that I truly can get through anything with Him. I realize the importance of my story now and not being scared of being judged. My story is of hope! I am now thriving, not just surviving in my life! God blessed me with a second chance, and I am using it to be a servant leader. My story matters; your story matters!

## Dennis's Story

My name is Dennis Otto. I lived in the darkness of drug addiction, sex, and violence for 30 years. I was sentenced to 110 months in prison. Because of my Savior Jesus Christ I now live in the light. This is my story.

I grew up in a fairly well-to-do family. I have four sisters and a brother. My mom stayed at home and raised our family while my dad worked to provide. My parents were very devout Catholics and that is how I was raised. I never took it no matter how many times I was forced to go to church. My dad never talked about Jesus or God at home. It was just always "Go to church." So at a very early age I was totally turned off by religion.

I started to drink alcohol that I had stolen from my parents at 14 years of age. Soon after, I was smoking weed. From the beginning, I always had to do more. More weed and booze, and soon after every type of drug. You name it and I did it. Immediately I started having problems with my parents. My dad and I were fighting constantly and many times physically. At 17, I graduated from high school and started to work construction. I moved out shortly after. At this time I started getting in trouble with the law, some fighting (assaults) and a DWI. At 19, the judge in our small town was getting pretty tired of seeing me in his courtroom, so I decided to move. I headed to the east side of St. Paul.

In St. Paul I started to run with some pretty serious dudes. At 19, I started to deal in cocaine. Now I really found my niche. Soon I was also dealing weed, acid, and speed. But coke was my main drug. It was the early 80's and life was one big party. I was hanging with some pretty serious people and was getting picked up by the law on some serious suspicions. I was never charged which made me even bolder. Through all this, women came and went until I got one of them pregnant. This was a wake-up call. After my son was born, a couple of my buddies got picked up on murder one. I realized I needed to do things differently for my son. We moved to a small town out in the country and lived a fairly normal life. I quit dealing, and drug use became occasional.

I was working construction and bought a house. I had another boy and girl, but the marriage was over. I found out that my wife was sleeping around. I found out my four-year-old daughter wasn't even mine. My world came crashing down. I thought that I had a good marriage, a nice house, I was working hard, the works. . . . I never saw it coming.

Just so you know, my daughter might not have my DNA but she is MY daughter. My wife and three children moved in with her new boyfriend. Not my daughter's biological dad, another guy. I was hurting like never before.

I started drinking heavily and my drug use skyrocketed. Soon I was back dealing. It was the early 90's and meth started to become popular. The next thing you know, you are manufacturing meth. I started to run with a "1% outlaw" motorcycle club. Now things started to get really crazy. Women, drugs, guns, and violence ran rampant. It was all a daily occurrence. In the year 2001, I came on the radar of the county drug task force. A couple of years later I am sentenced to a 110 months in prison. Charges were first-degree manufacturing and first-degree distribution. Through all this I started to see how much my family loved me. My dad never left me. I was released after 42 months because I went through the prison boot camp program. It was a good thing because my first year out, I was under such close supervision that I had to behave. Part of my early release terms was that I had to go to NA (Narcotics Anonymous). I met some good people including my wife Patti. But, I never worked the NA program. I went to meetings because I had to and also to meet people. My relationship at this point with my kids and dad were great so I made a decision to stay clean and out of trouble. It was tough.

I was 48 years old, broke, and all my old friends were a thing of my past. I was working for a nonunion construction company and making peanuts. It was so tempting to just make a batch of meth and make some quick cash. But I didn't. I was trying to be a better man but struggled with my anger and aggressive behavior. I was so empty on the inside and had no clue why. I was dating Patti for about a year when she became pregnant. Now I am 50 years old and have a little boy. I was determined to be a good dad. Patti and our son moved in with me; money was tight, but things were going pretty good.

Something was still missing in my life. So a few weeks after being released from prison I am out to eat with Patti's family when I am approached by Patti's brother-in-law. He asked me where I was at spiritually. I looked at him thinking that this was kind of weird. Then I answered saying I have been living in hell for most of my life. I hope that when I die it is better than this. So we talked. He asked what I thought of God and Jesus. I told him I wasn't sure if there was a God. After things I have seen and done, I couldn't see how there could be a God. At the end he asked if I would read a book if he gave it to me. I agreed to it. The book is *One Heartbeat Away* by Mark Cahill. I read this book about Jesus and things just started to click. At the end, I went right to my knees and asked Jesus to forgive me. This was March 15, 2010.

Before, whenever I heard the phrase "born again Christian," I always thought "yeah, right." Well, let me tell you, I was born again! All of a sudden it was like I was seeing the world for the first time. I was on fire for Jesus! I got plugged into a great church and within a month was in their Alpha course. This is teaching about Christianity. I was asked and agreed to giving my video testimonial to all the church campuses. I began to do service work to the church. I was ushering and meeting so many good people. Do you know how amazing it is to have true friends for the first time in my life? I was changing; I felt alive. Yes, I still had money problems. I also knew Jesus forgave me, but I was having trouble forgiving myself. I could now see how God was watching over me. He was protecting me even when I didn't know Him.

One night one of the pastors from church wanted to meet with Patti and me. He asked about our relationship. I told him we were going to get married when we could afford it. Well, needless to say, he called us out on it. That night Patti and I decided to get married, and we were—28 days later. As soon as we took that sin out of our lives, things really started to change. I got a new union job, bills got paid, and most importantly I felt closer than ever to God.

Patti became pregnant again. So, now at the age of 53, I have a newborn son and a three-year-old. I am now raising these boys in a Christian home. I was able to buy a house a year and a half ago. I am also talking to my three older kids about Jesus, too. They see the changes that Jesus has made in me. They believe in Jesus but just haven't taken the step to follow Him yet. I keep praying. Because of Jesus I feel so free from my past. I am not shy about it though. It made me who I am today. I went to Peru on a mission trip in January of 2014. A bunch of guys from church went up the Amazon River to a remote village in the jungle. We built them a church that they had been praying for the last five years. I do all I can do to give back. God has blessed me in so many ways. I feel the need to help others. I am now a part of the "Hope 360 Ministry." My story is on the web and anyone can get ahold of me through this website. I will talk to anyone and try to help. If Jesus can change a man like me, there is hope for anyone. If my past story can bring just one person to Jesus, then everything I went through was worth it. God Bless.

## Derek's Story

Standing in my living room dizzily looking around me one afternoon, taking in all that I had accomplished and reflecting on what I had acquired; the big screen on the wall, the luxury car and boat in the driveway, and the manicured landscape of our second home in one of the most beautiful areas in the country, I felt utter despair. At thirty-one years old I was the CEO of a growing company, had a beautiful and intelligent wife and had what most people would call a dream lifestyle, and that's exactly what I felt that I was in, a bad dream. At that moment everything in my life changed in one simple thought: *this was as good as it would ever get, this is all my life will amount to unless I change.* The next thought was equally as powerful in creating what would become the biggest change in my life: *I'll be lucky if things stay this good, they'll most likely get worse if I don't change.* I was a functioning alcoholic that couldn't go more than a few hours without a drink, and I used cocaine on a daily basis.

I had grown up in a good home with loving and faithful parents who had worked hard to provide for my brother and me. They had taken advantage of one of the great attributes of American society and lifted our family from a state of near poverty to comfortable middle class. I admired my parents immensely for this, their work ethic and dedication to being good parents. They had set a good model for us in so many ways, and yet I see now that they had also passed on another less ideal identity to me—they were alcoholics and had been for most of my life. The impact of growing up with alcoholic parents can't be measured. Its effects differ from child to child and the results can range from depression, anger, and detachment to what happened for me—creating a pattern that is repeated as that child grows.

I started drinking in junior high school, stealing bottles of Kessler's Whiskey from my friend's father's house and stashing it in the bushes at the corner of the track where we would run laps during P.E. class. Our teacher was somewhat elderly (we called him Old Man Peterson) and not the most astute and didn't happen to notice when I would hide at the back of the pack during warm-up laps, and when we came to my corner I would dip out, hide in the bushes, and enjoy a few nips off the bottle. This was the beginning of a sixteen year love affair with my best friend and my worst enemy all wrapped up in one—booze. Over the next decade and a half I would be scarred in bar fights, survive catastrophic high speed car crashes, nearly die from overdose, and destroy many relationships, all while maintaining the lifestyle that kept up the image that I was "normal."

I believe that all of us are put in this world for a purpose, *a reason for being,* and when this purpose is not being realized or acted upon, it creates a sadness and a hole right through the middle of us. I had been living for this feeling for years, and the only solution I knew of was to drink and use drugs, which paradoxically was only perpetuating the very despair I was trying to escape. In the despair I found one other solace I could turn to, it was to rely on the faith that I was raised with; and in an almost unconscious and automatic way, I began to pray. I prayed for one thing; some call it the prayer of desperation—I simply prayed for help. I was spiritually and morally bankrupt, and the one thing I had, my word, was worthless and I needed something, anything.

The interesting thing is that during the time when I was praying, sometimes in tears, things didn't get better; they actually got worse. I realize now that this was a blessing from God because it was necessary for me to reach my bottom—that place where there is nowhere to go but up, even if that means death. That place came to me in the form of being asked by the president of my company to either get clean and sober or resign from my position and employment because no one wanted to work with who I had become. After all that I had been through, this was the thing that I couldn't accept. Looking back, I guess it's because my identity was threatened, my ego wouldn't let me become "unsuccessful' and jobless. They offered to pay for a thirty-day rehab or they would support me in attending Alcoholics Anonymous for a minimum of ninety meetings in ninety days. I attended a meeting the very next morning and began the second half of my life and the answer to my prayers was revealed.

I found quickly that AA was not about a bunch of pitiful drunks commiserating and getting together to relive their glory days as I had imagined it was. AA is a spiritual program based in biblical principles, and it reintroduced me to God, the God whom I had been praying to and the only answer to my problems. I didn't realize it then, but that day in my living room I had begun to *surrender*. I had become *willing*. At the core of the AA principle is to turn one's life and will over to the care of God or simply put—faith. As I followed the steps, working with someone who had what I wanted, what we call a sponsor, I started to feel the sweet freedom from resentment, regret, and guilt. My life began to open up before me, and I had hope for the first time in a long time. During this time, I not only diligently followed the program that had worked for thousands before me but I also started to read the Bible, the ultimate self-help book. I remember clearly coming across a verse one early morning that I didn't fully understand at the time but that would set me on a course to living my purpose.

*"And now these three remain; Faith, Hope and Love and the greatest of these is Love."*

1 Corinthians 13:13 was like a seed planted in my heart and watered with my constant thought; I pondered this daily and let God reveal His meaning for me in it. Over time, I began to realize that this was the roadmap for my new life, that my life would be dedicated to love. I knew what love felt like, but I couldn't figure out what love looked like until it dawned on me—the verb for love is *service.* Love is giving, love is without judgment, and love is by nature unconditional. I set out to live each day to be of the greatest service to as many people as possible. If I had been suffering from a disease of self-centered fear, this was the ultimate solution. I began to wake up each morning and turn my life over to the will of God in prayer and meditation. My life began to change in indescribable ways as I was led to people and circumstances that allowed me to start living that purpose that I was born for—to inspire others to have vision for their life, believe in themselves, and take action based in that belief. I'm grateful for all that I've been through and that it can be a testimony to others that when we turn to God, we are never let down and we are graciously cared for as His children. Be willing to grow, have faith in the God of your understanding, accept His will for you, and be grateful for what shows up. And your life will become what you dream it to be.

Today I have over seven years of continuous sobriety, and my life is filled each day with passion and purpose. I have more of the great blessings than I ever dreamed I would. My wife, who is the angel that has stood by my side for nearly fifteen years (even during the times when she was afraid to have children with me because of the way I lived) is now my partner in business and in raising our two greatest gifts—our four and five-year-old sons Henry and Lucas. Together, Corrina and I spend our days working from our beautiful home in the redwood trees near the California coast, joyously giving all of ourselves to our family, friends, and to as many new people as God brings our way. I sit back and smile as I realize that my life, down to the smallest detail, is now exactly what I pictured in my mind that it could someday be back when I first decided to start living for others instead of myself.

---

Hopefully the stories of Tony, Dennis, and Derek show the two common threads: first, they were all at the end of their rope or the "bottom" as they say; and second, God alone was the source of their intervention. It is impossible for man to save himself, and this has become very obvious to me over my 20-year journey to learn the truth. The one and only true answer is being redeemed by God.

If you are currently struggling with this disease, understand it is terminal, but with God's intervention, your true repentance (turning 180 degrees away from where you are headed), you will be able to manage the disease.

If you have a child, mate, family member, or friend in this terminal tunnel, do not enable them; do not allow them to drag you into the tunnel they have created. Simply know that **God** is in control, **rejoice** knowing this is in God's hands, and eliminate the stress by **initiating** your faith (believing something is so, when it's not so, so it can be so), have faith in the positive outcome, and finally **pray** for wisdom. Yes, **GRIP.** Do not get caught in the emotional prayers of "Why me God? How can you do this to me God? God, take this thorn from my flesh!" No, your prayer is "God, give me the wisdom to understand how to handle this situation. Bring those to me who have been through the tunnel and can give me input on how to remain strong during this trial."

My friends, learn about this disease and understand that those who are affected are the world's biggest liars, and they will lie with such conviction. They will be sincere when they say that they have no problem and don't associate with those who have the problem. If the affected child is young, don't preach but teach. Be equipped and let them know you have the facts. Let them understand the consequences—not based upon emotion but upon concrete evidence (you can find great data on Google). Share with your young kids that they are responsible for their actions and the privileges you grant them (phones, access to music, friends, etc.). Help them understand that they will be lost if they use drugs and alcohol. If they don't heed your warnings, continue the behavior, violate principles and laws, and land in jail, **do not** bail them out! Let them stay for as long as the judge demands! The child must understand he/she is responsible for their choices.

Finally, know that none of this shocks God. He sees it, He knows the outcome, He is in total control, and all things are under His authority:

> For the Scriptures say, "God has put all things
> under his authority." (1 Corinthians 15:27)

This challenge is not so much about your loved one as it is about **you**! This test is to see how fast you run to the foot of the cross and give it all to God. This is about **you** and **your** relationship with God. This is about how strongly you believe in God's sovereignty. This is about **you** resting in the Word of God and the truth of His Word. This tunnel, like all previous tunnels and future tunnels, is about whether or not you have a **GRIP!**

Footnote: It has now been several months since my son has had a drink. He is doing very well through God's grace and favor and is working diligently to remain strong in the Lord. We are so proud of him.

# 11

# THE FINAL TUNNEL

*"Bobby, I have figured this whole thing out; we are not getting out of here alive."* Zig Ziglar

I shared this quote earlier in the book, but as I write this final chapter, the words from my friend Mr. Zig still ring in my ears. Zig was a great friend and mentor, but most important, he was a sincere believer in Jesus. If you spent any length of time with Mr. Zig, you would hear about Jesus and the value he placed on the Bible.

I am confident that some reading this might be in the final chapter of life. Some of you are Christ-followers, and (like me) you believe in the fact that there is a better place after death than the one we occupy during our current lives. For the sake of those readers who are not Christ-followers, I want to end this book where I began—with the gospel of Jesus. As I Google the word "death" in the Bible, there are 460 results found in the translation I am using. There are some very promising words associated with the believer, you and I who have turned our lives over to Christ.

> *"There is more than enough room in my Father's home. If this were not so, would I have told you that I am going to prepare a place for you? When everything is ready, I will come and get you, so that you will always be with me where I am." (John 14:2-3)*

What jumps out to me are the words **"when everything is ready, I will come and get you."** So I need to ask you, my readers, today can you say "I am ready!" Do you know without any reservation should you die this very moment that you will be in heaven for all of eternity? My friends, if you take nothing else from this book, please hear my words that it is possible to live with Christ in eternity. The decision was mine, the decision is yours today, simply acknowledge that Jesus Christ is Lord, that you totally surrender your life to Him, and that you will repent by changing your direction in life to live according to His Word. It's not rocket science; there is no way you can work your way to heaven, give your way to heaven, or get there just by being a good person. Living the eternal life with Christ is a gift, and it comes by grace not works.

> "God saved you by his grace when you believed. And you can't take credit for this; it is a gift from God. Salvation is not a reward for the good things we have done, so none of us can boast about it." (Ephesians 2:8-9)

I have found so many folks working hard to enter heaven. Many churches teach that you can only get to heaven by working or that you can gain a special place in heaven depending on how much you work on earth. My friends, we are saved by **grace** so that we can't take the credit and boast. I was saved by grace, and the Holy Spirit within me has created a heart that wants to produce good works here on earth, but that has nothing to do with my personal salvation. If you are in the final tunnel facing death, call on the name of the Lord Jesus Christ, and let His grace abound in you. If you make this final decision prior to your departure, then heaven's door will be open for you.

In addition to our salvation, we can have the "confident hope" that until we enter heaven, God is for us and with us here on earth during all of our tunnel times.

> *"And we know that God causes everything* [all our tunnels] *to work together for the good of those who love God* [that would be you] *and are called according to his purpose for them."* *(Romans 8:28)*

My friends, no one reading this is immune to "tunnel times," but let us remember:

> *Weeping may last through the night, but joy comes with the morning. (Psalm 30:5)*

Your tunnels will not last forever! Have "confident hope" that joy is coming.

## Staying on the Track

*"You can be on the right track but if you're not moving, you will be run over."* Will Rogers

---

As we close this book, I would like to share a few simple thoughts that have helped me stay on track over my 43 years of following Christ.

I started this book talking about the long railroad track of life. As we proceed down this track, overseen by the Master—traveling in and out of our many tunnels—there are some key lessons we can acknowledge and begin putting into practice. We must realize that we can never live on what we have learned alone, but we must always be progressing, learning new principles, and thinking new thoughts that will give us a greater ability to function at full speed through our future tunnels.

Remember, we can't coast until we enter our next tunnel, but the time that we have between each tunnel is our time to prepare for the next one. It is easy to forget the lessons we learn in the tunnel when life smooths out on the other side, to forget how desperately we needed God and what it was like to feel close to Him in the middle of our pain. The children of Israel had the same tendency—to forget what they learned in their wilderness tunnel.

> *Remember how the LORD your God led you through the wilderness* [the tunnel] *for these forty years, humbling you and testing you to prove your character, and to find out whether or not you would obey his commands. (Deuteronomy 8:2)*

> *For when you have become full and prosperous and have built fine homes to live in, and when your flocks and herds have become very large and your silver and gold have multiplied along with everything else, be careful! (Deuteronomy 8:12)*

Their tunnel time was "Egypt time" and "wilderness time," and after all that, they got fat and lazy on the other side forgetting the miracles God performed to pull them through.

What we read, who we associate with, and what we listen to dictates our ability to withstand the next tunnel. The best way to maximize our preparedness between tunnels is to read the Word of God—internalize His words, observe and absorb the truth so that we are spiritually equipped when we move into the darkness.

What can we glean from the Bible that can give us the faith to endure, the passion to prevail, and the strength to sustain in our future tunnels? The Word is our only tool from God that makes it possible to understand His will for our lives, and if we read it with an open heart asking the Holy Spirit to teach us, the Word can give us the instructions we need to endure the challenges we will certainly face.

Observe the typical response of people in the world when they enter their tunnels, and it doesn't take long to see why many never come out of the tunnel in one piece or how they come out being bitter, hateful, and cynical. When I speak of those in the world, I may be talking about many of the people in your current immediate circle. If you are a Christ-follower, you likely are in relationships with many who don't follow Him. It is easy to begin to listen to their worldly advice. This association can taint your biblical perspective, and if you're not careful, you will be less likely to live in obedience to Christ.

*Walk with the wise and become wise; associate*
*with fools and get in trouble. (Proverbs 13:20)*

There are so many choices to make, especially for some of my younger friends reading this book. The world and many of your friends say you should enjoy drugs and alcohol and party while you can; you're only young once. The world says go ahead and get a divorce; leave that person and find another because you know you will be happier. The world says, "Just declare bankruptcy and forget about those you owe money to. After all, they should have known better than to loan it to you!" And the world says, "Live only for yourself!" If you are a Christ-follower and are hanging around those who favor the world over God's favor, then you will be caught up in the rhetoric and drama, and just like a frog in lukewarm water, you will soon find yourself in hot water that you cannot escape.

I totally accept that Jesus came for the sick—not the healthy, for the sinner—not the saint, but I have found nowhere in the Bible where God set up camp for days, weeks, months, and years with the enemy in order to share the Good News. So beware who you are listening to when you enter the tunnels of life, for human wisdom isn't even close to the wisdom from the Word of God.

Next, read the Word daily; find the translation that brings the Scriptures to life, but read. Kay and I have made it a habit to read each morning during breakfast, and since we are on the road often, we have Bible Gateway in our smart phones.

This cool app takes you through the Bible with a daily reading. Each morning, a chapter or several verses appears in your phone. We have found it very helpful to read while we have breakfast each morning. Since I am a baby-boomer, I still must have my written Bible, for I love to highlight the scriptures God shows me that can help my life skills. It is amazing how many people around the world pay for a "life coach" when the greatest Coach that ever lived is "free." His words and wisdom jump from page to page in the Bible.

Remember, the books that you have read and the people you have chosen to be around will determine your growth in life, so this might be a great time to take inventory of what you are reading and who you are hanging around with.

During the past 40 years, I have spoken to over three million people and traveled over four million air miles; I've shared my message in coliseums of 30,000 people and in modest rooms with an audience of two. During this time, I am consistently asked which books I recommend and which scriptures I would suggest that would improve one's life skills.

I am very cautious about recommending books by men and women authors who have not stood the test of time, so

I have a pretty short list. I prefer to read those whose lives and writings have a record of integrity. Realizing that all ethics must be based on spiritual principles, I can recommend the following authors. I am confident there are likely thousands more I have not met or studied, but these I have. I assure you, if you buy every book each of these folks have written, you will have more than enough information for a lifetime, and you will never run out of reading material.

Each of these men and women, some living and some now deceased, based all their teaching on God's truth, and each had a profound impact on me.

Zig Ziglar

John Maxwell

Josh McDowell

Ken Blanchard

Mary Kay Ash

Billy Graham

Chuck Swindoll

John Blanchard (English evangelist)

Max Lucado

You may not be familiar with these names, but these are the men and women who have added value to my life.

I do not know many of them, but they all have lifted my life and soul as they shared written words of truth. Remember what I shared earlier: we become a product of the books we read and the people we associate with. If you will look back over your past five years, you will see that your life today is a result of those two influences. I challenge each of you to begin reading every book you can by the writers I've suggested. Highlight the truth they share; it will dramatically impact your life for the better.

## Basic Truth

This section is for my grandchildren and for those who want simple wisdom and truth—what I call life lessons. Over my years, I have taught leadership skills to millions predicated on the following words and thoughts. Life is not complicated if you have the correct set of values and follow simple truth. Much of my teaching comes from the book of Proverbs. Realizing that many people have translations that make the Bible seem a little complicated or confusing, I wanted to share the scriptures from my favorite translation (Tyndale NLT).

This translation makes it quite simple to understand basic but profound truth, words that have guided my thoughts and direction through 47 years of marriage and multiple business enterprises, words on creating relationships, guidance in raising three children and now six grandchildren. I have used these principles in teaching leadership worldwide from Fortune 100 companies to the US Army for over four decades. I have found over my years that people make life so complicated, and sadly, many of those are even professing Christ-followers. I am not sure how many will actually read the following words that have given me a favorable life with the Lord, but hopefully my wonderful grandkids will take the time after their Papi is gone to reflect on what kept him excited about living, having a wonderful marriage, and being successful in business for all these years. Caleb Chase, Kyleigh Dawn, McKenzie Elizabeth, Mikayla Dawn, Alexia McKay, and Allison Kate . . . listen to these words from Proverbs, and your lives will be filled with joy. Read a few of these words each day for the rest of your lives and experience the joy and peace that you so deserve.

*Grandchildren are the crowning glory of the aged; parents are the pride of their children. (Proverbs 17:6)*

### From Proverbs 1

**1:4** *These proverbs will give insight to the simple, knowledge and discernment to the young.*

**1:7** *Fear of the LORD is the foundation of true knowledge.*

**1:32** *Fools are destroyed by their own complacency.*

### From Proverbs 3

**3:5** *Trust in the LORD with all your heart; do not depend on your own understanding.*

**3:6** *Seek his will in all you do, and he will show you which path to take.*

*3:7  Don't be impressed with your own wisdom.*

*3:9-10  Honor the LORD with your wealth and with the best part of everything you produce. Then he will fill your barns with grain, and your vats will overflow with good wine*

*3:21  My child, don't lose sight of common sense and discernment. Hang on to them.*

## From Proverbs 4

*4:7  Getting wisdom is the wisest thing you can do! And whatever else you do, develop good judgment.*

*4:23  Guard your heart above all else, for it determines the course of your life.*

*4:24  Avoid all perverse talk; stay away from corrupt speech.*

*4:25  Look straight ahead, and fix your eyes on what lies before you.*

## From Proverbs 5

*5:22-23  An evil man . . . will die for lack of self-control; he will be lost because of his great foolishness.*

## From Proverbs 8 (Regarding Wisdom)

*8:17  I love all who love me. Those who search will surely find me.*

*8:21  Those who love me inherit wealth. I will fill their treasuries.*

*8:35  For whoever finds me finds life and receives favor from the LORD.*

## From Proverbs 9

**9:9** *Instruct the wise, and they will be even wiser.*

## From Proverbs 10

**10:4** *Lazy people are soon poor; hard workers get rich.*

**10:16** *The earnings of the godly enhance their lives, but evil people squander their money on sin.*

**10:17** *People who accept discipline are on the pathway to life, but those who ignore correction will go astray.*

**10:19** *Too much talk lead to sin. Be sensible and keep your mouth shut.*

**10:21** *The words of the godly encourage many, but fools are destroyed by their lack of common sense.*

## From Proverbs 11

**11:2** *Pride leads to disgrace, but with humility comes wisdom.*
**11:14** *Without wise leadership, a nation falls; there is safety in having many advisers.*

**11:24** *Give freely and become more wealthy; be stingy and lose everything.*

**11:25** *The generous will prosper; those who refresh others will themselves be refreshed.*

## From Proverbs 12

**12:11**  *A hard worker has plenty of food, but a person who chases fantasies has no sense.*

**12:16**  *A fool is quick-tempered, but a wise person stays calm when insulted.*

**12:24**  *Work hard and become a leader; be lazy and become a slave.*

**12:25**  *Worry weighs a person down; an encouraging word cheers a person up.*

## From Proverbs 13

**13:3**  *Those who control their tongue will have a long life; opening your mouth can ruin everything.*

**13:4**  *Lazy people want much but get little, but those who work hard will prosper.*

**13:7**  *Some who are poor pretend to be rich; others who are rich pretend to be poor.*

**13:20**  *Walk with the wise and become wise; associate with fools and get in trouble.*

**13:24**  *Those who spare the rod of discipline hate their children. Those who love their children care enough to discipline them.*

### From Proverbs 14

**14:23** *Work brings profit, but mere talk leads to poverty!*

**14:29** *People with understanding control their anger; a hot temper shows great foolishness.*

### From Proverbs 15

**15:1** *A gentle answer deflects anger, but harsh words make tempers flare.*

**15:22** *Plans go wrong for lack of advice; many advisers bring success.*

### From Proverbs 16

**16:3** *Commit your actions to the LORD, and your plans will succeed.*

**16:4** *The LORD has made everything for his own purposes, even the wicked for a day of disaster.*

**16:5** *The LORD detests the proud; they will surely be punished.*

**16:9** *We can make our plans, but the LORD determines our steps.*

**16:18** *Pride goes before destruction, and haughtiness before a fall.*

**16:23** *From a wise mind comes wise speech; the words of the wise are persuasive*

**16:24** *Kind words are like honey—sweet to the soul and healthy for the body.*

**16:32**  *Better to be patient than powerful; better to have self control than to conquer a city.*

**16:33**  *We may throw the dice, but the LORD determines how they fall.*

## From Proverbs 17

**17:14**  *Starting a quarrel is like opening a floodgate, so stop before a dispute breaks out.*

**17:21**  *It is painful to be the parent of a fool; there is no joy for the father of a rebel.*

**17:22**  *A cheerful heart is good medicine, but a broken spirit saps a person's strength.*

**17:27**  *A truly wise person uses few words; a person with understanding is even-tempered.*

**17:28**  *Even fools are thought wise when they keep silent; with their mouths shut, they seem intelligent.*

## From Proverbs 18

**18:13**  *Spouting off before listening to the facts is both shameful and foolish.*

**18:15**  *Intelligent people are always ready to learn. Their ears are open for knowledge.*

### From Proverbs 19

**19:3** *People ruin their lives by their own foolishness and then are angry at the LORD.*

**19:11** *Sensible people control their temper; they earn respect by overlooking wrongs.*

### From Proverbs 20

**20:20** *If you insult your father or mother, your light will be snuffed out in total darkness.*

**20:22** *Don't say, "I will get even for this wrong." Wait for the LORD to handle the matter.*

**20:24** *The LORD directs our steps, so why try to understand everything along the way?*

### From Proverbs 21

**21:1** *The king's heart is like a stream of water directed by the LORD; he guides it wherever he pleases.*

**21:5** *Good planning and hard work lead to prosperity, but hasty shortcuts lead to poverty.*

**21:13** *Those who shut their ears to the cries of the poor will be ignored in their own time of need.*

**21:20** *The wise have wealth and luxury, but fools spend whatever they get.*

**21:23** *Watch your tongue and keep your mouth shut, and you will stay out of trouble.*

**21:25** *Despite their desires, the lazy will come to ruin, for their hands refuse to work.*

### From Proverbs 22

**22:4** *True humility and fear of the LORD lead to riches, honor, and long life.*

**22:9** *Blessed are those who are generous, because they feed the poor.*

### From Proverbs 23

**23:4** *Don't wear yourself out trying to get rich. Be wise enough to know when to quit.*

**23:5** *In the blink of an eye wealth disappears, for it will sprout wigs and fly away like an eagle.*

### From Proverbs 24

**24:10** *If you fail under pressure, your strength is too small.*

### From Proverbs 25

**25:23** *As surely as a north wind brings rain, so a gossiping tongue causes anger!*

### From Proverbs 26

**26:20** *Fire goes out without wood, and quarrels disappear when gossip stops.*

### From Proverbs 27

**27:1** *Don't brag about tomorrow, since you don't know what the day will bring.*

**27:2** *Let someone else praise you, not your own mouth.*

**27:17** *As iron sharpens iron, so a friend sharpens a friend.*

# AND SO TO CLOSE

I hope this book has helped you as you travel down the rails of life, knowing without a doubt that none of the tunnels you face will be a shock to God. In all of your tunnels, the faster you can get a **GRIP,** the faster the darkness of the tunnel will become light. When you internalize the truth that **God is sovereign,** that **rejoicing** reduces the stress, that **faith** will deliver, and wisdom from His Word and **prayer** will keep you focused, then life becomes enjoyable.

My request is that you don't keep these thoughts for yourself but that you share them. Give these words away; let your mate, family, and friends know that you now have a **GRIP** on your challenges and how they can get a **GRIP** as well.

I especially would like to ask that you send me an email at bob@bobgoshen.com and share how this book has enhanced your life. Feel free to share any tunnel experience you are encountering so I can lift you in my daily prayers. If you wish to have better clarity on how to know Christ as your personal savior, send me your telephone number, and I will give you a personal call.

I hope we can meet someday as I travel the globe speaking, but if not, I will look forward to the day we all meet in heaven.

---Bob Goshen

# ABOUT THE AUTHOR

Bob Goshen has logged more than 4 million air miles traveling the world sharing leadership and personal development skills. He has delivered over 4,000 presentations, and whether he is speaking in a coliseum to more than 30,000 people or participating in a simple one-on-one discussion, Bob's message is unwavering—you are where you are and you are who you are as the result of God's sovereign hand and His favor. His clear message is that "God has a purpose and plan for your life, and He has yet to call anyone who He has not equipped." He shares that life is more often a battle than beautiful, that you will be going in and out of dark tunnels your entire life, but it is how you equip yourself between the tunnels that creates the Godly character required to live and eventually die for Christ.

Bob and his beautiful wife Kay have had many personal tunnel times during their almost 50 years of marriage, and they share this book not from head knowledge but from the heart. Having raised three wonderful kids who've given them six adorable grandkids, their calling remains as they share "God has a plan" so "Get a GRIP."

**To have Bob come and share with your organization, email Bob at bob@bobgoshen.com**